I0115943

The Gentleman's Guide to Understanding Cheating

An Incisive Look at Infidelity in the

Modern Era:

Ethics, Methods, Means, and Dangers

By Joseph Sebastian

Copyright © 2017 Joseph Sebastian

Table of Contents

So You're Going To Cheat 1

    The legality of infidelity 1

    The ethics of infidelity 2

    Why do men cheat? 4

    Alternatives.. 12

    Summary 18

Know the Objective **20**

    The science...20

    How to get the woman you don't want...........................26

    Women aren't crazy, but the ones you meet may be......29

The Rules **32**

    Don't get caught...32

    Don't confess...32

    Your lover is a person 32

Presenting Yourself.......................................**34**

    Appearance and grooming.....................................35

    Culture..38

    Conversation 39

    Manners 49

    Be Valuable...53

    Decide who you are 55

    Your Options...56

Know your environments **65**

    Target environments..66

How your affair will look....................................77

    Patterns of typical affairs............................77

The Technical Details.............................82

    Method acting...............................82

    The excuse....................................85

    Supplementary material - mail, etc.............95

    Sanitize..98

    Electronic Sanitation 105

    Occasionally fake a crisis...................114

    Check her alibi................................114

    Finances..116

Dangers/Pitfalls 120

    Your guilt......................................120

    Scent...125

    Lube..126

    Third parties..................................127

    Birth control..................................128

    Disease 131

    Jealousy.......................................138

    Marking.......................................139

    Easily checked deceptions 141

    Emergencies..................................143

    Devices...145

    Know the divorce laws.....................146

Down the road 148

    The long game 148

Your wife 149

Glaciation 151

Checklists and Conclusion 1

Readiness checklist 1

Per date checklist 1

Conclusion 2

Review Us 3

So You're Going To Cheat

If you're reading this book, you are either already cheating and feel in need of guidance, or you are seriously contemplating cheating.

Before we get started, we're going to ask you to think about some things. Maybe you don't need to. You may already be in the middle of an affair and just want help managing it. If that's you, then it might be useful to read along anyway in case it raises some questions on whether or not cheating is a good idea. If not, skip ahead to the Technical section for the "how to" details.

The legality of infidelity

Cheating between consenting adults is effectively legal in the United States for civilians. A few states still maintain clauses punishing adultery, but Lawrence v. Texas, 539 U.S. 558 (2003), the Supreme Court case which struck down sodomy laws, is generally understood to have invalidated them. A test case in Virginia, Martin v. Ziherl, 269 Va. 35, 42 (2005), cited Lawrence, and did not uphold Virginia Law in the case of consenting adults. It is beyond unlikely for any police outside of a small rural jurisdiction to consider an adultery charge.

Legality within the Military

Within the military it may come under various regulations and laws regarding conduct. The military has a wide range of latitude regarding regulations. Writing in Slate in December 2003, Brendan Koerner tells us that: "Proving adultery under military guidelines is no mean prosecutorial feat. According to Article 134 of the Uniform Code of Military Justice (UCMJ), the prosecution must prove that the accused not only committed the indiscretion, but also that his or her conduct 'was to the prejudice of good order and discipline in the armed forces or was of a nature to bring discredit upon the armed forces.' In other words, the affair must somehow have hampered the military's ability to do its job—say, by lowering morale on a base, or by damaging the public's faith in the armed forces."

Military members charged with adultery can face up to a year in confinement and dishonorable discharge, which means forfeiting retirement pay. That said, prosecutions are extremely unusual except when they involve the spouses of other members of the same military unit or other highly prejudicial elements.

The military has not revised Article 134 since Lawrence, and the invalidation of the first two elements under US law would not necessarily invalidate the "prejudice to good order" element. The UCMJ does not have to be in compliance with the Constitution, as it is a special contract created by the Oath of Enlistment.

The ethics of infidelity

In movies and books men and women both are "evil cheaters." They are wrongdoers out to deceive people for their own carnal gain. Reality is a bit more complex. People cheat for a variety of reasons.

Many scientists believe that monogamy may not be a particularly natural state for human beings. Writing in their book *Sex at Dawn* Christopher Ryan PhD and Cacilda Jethá MD suggest that lifelong marriage is not an evolutionary norm for human beings, but an economic encumberment that came with the dawn of agriculture. Certainly all humans who have children "mate" and "pair bond" at least briefly, but their investigations reject the idea that monogamous marriage is an instinctive human norm.

They conclude: "many qualities considered essential components of marriage in contemporary Western usage are anything but universal: sexual exclusivity, property exchange, even the intention to stay together for long. None of these are expected in many of the relationships evolutionary psychologists and anthropologists insist on calling marriage."

In Ryan and Jetha's view, lifelong monogamous marriage is no more "fundamental" to human beings than working 9-5 at a desk in an office tower, and many humans may feel trapped by a system which does not meet their needs.

American Sociologist Eric Anderson, author of *The Monogamy Gap: Men, Love, and the Reality of Cheating* goes further calling monogamy "socially compelled sexual incarceration" and linking it to anger and contempt for our partners.

A study by Joan Atwood and Limor Schwartz around 2000 reviewed many studies to suggest about "50-60% of married men and 45-55% of married women engage in extramarital sex at some time or another during their marriage and almost half come to therapy because of it."

If infidelity to a single partner is a condition common to half the human race, and a quarter of them require therapy, maybe the problem isn't their urges to cheat, but the narrow system in which they are forced to live.

Cheating outside of marriage

If you're cheating, but have never tied the knot, great. Almost everything in this book applies to any long term relationship, particularly a live-in relationship. It just gets a little easier. But pay attention all the same. You'll find more similarities than differences.

Terms for this book

Throughout this book we're going to use the terms "spouse" or "wife" to refer to your long term partner, the person you are cheating *on*. "Partner" will typically refer to the person you are cheating *with*. This isn't meant to imply that is always the arrangement, but it helps keep things sorted out, and avoids a lot of extra words.

Why do men cheat?

This may be the most common cover tease in the history of women's magazines, and most any article you can find is written with the presumption that cheaters are bad, flawed, or immature. Not surprisingly the answers are far more complicated.

Now maybe you're saying "what does it matter why I cheat...move along here!" We think it does matter.

If you were a General asked by the President to carry out a military operation, you would want to know the actual objective. "Invade North Korea" is vague. "Invade North Korea and depose the Dictator" is a very different mission from "Attack North Korea and seize a dangerous missile complex, destroying the technology there." The two operations call for very different plans. If you don't know why you want to cheat, you aren't likely to end up in a situation that meets your needs with minimal harm to your life.

Many men don't want to think about the reasons they want to cheat. Like a Catholic schoolgirl who ends up pregnant at 18 because she didn't carry a condom since it would mean she was "planning to have sex," they want to "fall into an affair" without thinking about the reasons. And like the schoolgirl, they often end up in big trouble.

You're an adult, not an 18 year old schoolgirl. You owe it to yourself, your happiness, and your partner, to think about the reasons you want to cheat. Here is a list based on various psychological sources, with the pejoratives removed. Note that you may find more than one of these pertains to you. Men seldom cheat for only one reason, usually there is a mixture of reasons.

Proving something

Five years ago, she could not get enough of you. She wanted you all the time. Now there's another baby on the way and the last time you had sex was last December. Or maybe she wants you, but only on her terms. She has a headache or not. You have to bring flowers, plead, lower yourself to get sex.

There are a million variations, but the end result is a man who wonders "do I still have it? Have I become a wet dishrag, a man nobody will ever desire."

Then there is the flash of a smile, the spark of interest and it's on. The need to prove "I still have it" wins out over any other concern.

Feeling undesirable can lead to depression, even physical problems. Cheating isn't the only alternative, and we'll talk later about some other options. But for some people it may be the only, practical, short term option.

The rush

Let's put the shoe on the other foot. Maybe it's you that puts off sex, and doesn't care when she puts on perfume, makes a nice dinner or tries to seduce you. You don't mean to hurt her you just don't feel excited. Dating was a rush, drove your pulse. Knowing you can have her any time you want just makes it hard to...get hard.

Remember what we said above. There's no proof that humans are "inherently" monogamous. In some men the sex drive may be heavily mixed up with dopamine, the neurochemical that makes us feel excited and rewarded. Think about playing a tough game, and winning. That afterglow? Dopamine. Think about getting the girl...the afterglow...dopamine.

You don't hate her, you don't want to leave her. You have a life together. But you cannot get excited. You're not a bad person. You're just not chemically wired for pair-bonding, or you're wired to be intimate, but not sexual, with a long term partner. Fighting your chemistry may leave you bitter and depleted. Many individuals who engage in domestic violence may be driven by a dopamine addiction to new partners, and become violent when they perceive their partner as a roadblock.

More than any other type, this requires some sort of long term fix. It isn't fair to put her up on a shelf while you play, and it certainly is not okay to become violent. Still, you may need some time and perspective, and in the short term, cheating may be the only route to figure out what you really want and need.

Feeling trapped

For all the power in our lives we are increasingly trapped. American men, in particular, are pressed to work far more hours than men abroad for the same quality of life, and we live in a culture that teaches us we are deficient if we don't have the latest thing. This used to be referred to as the "rat-race" but most of us today have grown up accepting it as "the way things are."

We struggle to find ourselves mired in a net of mortgage debt, student debt, auto debt, with unmanageable college tuition payments looming. Our spouse begins to seem like an extension of the Bank and the IRS, demanding money, time and attention.

Our spouse is not the one at fault, and on some level, at least hopefully, we know that. But we feel cornered and they are not in our corner. The desire to get out, to have something for ourselves, to prove we have the power to go beyond the prison walls of day to day becomes overwhelming.

Intimacy

Maybe you withdrew it first, or maybe she did, but the intimacy is gone. You are living with a stranger. Often children can bring this on. "My wife" an object of intimacy becomes "mom" whose intimacy is bestowed on the children. There is tenseness, bickering, and zero contact.

You used to share thoughts, dreams, hopes. Now you share barbs or accusations about who doesn't do enough of the chores. Intimacy is hard to maintain in adults who live together. The failure of intimacy may be an outgrowth for one or both of you of the issues we discussed above in "trapped."

Nonetheless you want to create a secret place of your own, lay with a lover on a pillow and whisper about all the things you have never had, all the depths in you. Often intimate cheating begins, or exists, entirely online, which leads to the phenomenon of the "emotional affair."

Sexual need

We didn't list this first, because cheating is most often not about sex. But sometimes it is. It's spring, you see the first girl with a short skirt showing legs and you would give your right arm for sex. The traditional book and movie picture of this is someone whose wife is "cold to him," but in fact sexual need may hit anyone. The desire for sex with someone, anyone, who isn't your primary partner.

Some of us may be wired to "spread it around." Research conducted at the College of Wooster in Ohio concluded that men exposed to a new partner "ejaculated at a faster rate with higher volumes of semen," than they did with a regular partner, leading Dr. Laura K. Sirot to conclude "the results of this study and other studies of human differential ejaculation behavior suggest that extra-pair (or extramarital) copulations may have occurred in our evolutionary past."

Dr. Sirot would not go so far as to say the relatively small study indicated that natural selection and our "natural" sex drives favored infidelity, but the fact she commented negatively makes it clear that there is a potential link.

Stories suggest men who are suddenly doing well find they have strong desires for another partner, often any partner. Some psychologists have suggested this is a natural reaction to abundance. The genetic imperative behind our sex drives is to perpetuate our genes through our sperm (even if we short circuit the process with modern technology) and it has been widely suggested that taking additional mates "on the side" especially when there are additional resources that tell our subconscious that we could feed additional children, is a key male reproductive strategy.

The good news? Men who take additional partners on the side may perform better with their primary partners too. This doesn't remove the social consequences of cheating, but it does make things a little less bleak.

A special subcategory of sexual desire is youth. Psychologists have thought for years that men were typically attracted to women much younger than themselves. This makes sense. Our biological drive is to sire children. Historically, maternal death and infant mortality were higher even than the third world rates prevalent in much of the United States today, and younger women were more likely to survive pregnancy, so men who tended to select younger partners had more children, which resulted in that preference being passed along.

The power

Let's get down to brass tacks. Sometimes it's just power. That sounds awful doesn't it? You want to have multiple people in your life, control them, have sex with them, have relationships with them, and have it all be about you.

Except, realistically this is just a positive framing of proving something or feeling trapped. Let's face it. Having multiple little worlds to yourself is just part of those concepts. But feeling that it's about you being powerful feels a little better than thinking it is about you escaping.

Experimental divorce

This is another category that's really a mashup, but it deserves its own heading. A lot of men have already more or less decided they are through with their relationship. The affair is not just an affair, it's a stepping stone. They can't imagine living on their own, even if they think they can, and even if they contemplate glorious bachelorhood, they want a set of arms to fall into, a shoulder to cry on, and a person to prepare hot food before they make the jump. They're scared to get divorced until they are certain that they can line up the next Mrs. Right.

This is a legitimate reason to experiment with affairs, but consider a few factors. First, you are going to be *very* emotionally beholden to Mrs. Next, even if you haven't promised an engagement "as soon as the divorce is final." As a bachelor you may get other offers and find yourself in a very bad position to act on them. You may be accepting someone of lower status and less satisfying than you really want, out of desperate need to get out of a situation that isn't working at all.

Getting kinky

One final reason that men seek affairs is that they "aren't getting what they need" from their wife. That can mean a lot of things. If you watch porn and see girls deep throating until they gag, and cheerfully spasming in orgasm while being anally penetrated, you may have the idea that your wife is underperforming. I've known men who literally sought an affair because they wanted oral.

Like many other sidelines that may be the focus of future titles in this line, full discussion of this is out of our range, however many men who conduct affairs do so in a kink/fetish context. If you're interested in being submissive, you may want to look at Sex Workers, below, and consider a professional domme or dominatrix. If you are interested in being the one on top, you'll have more luck on sites like Kink.com, but be aware you will need to build a significant layer of opacity between your normal and kinky life. The Fetish community tends to value openness and honesty, and men who are obviously cheating can have a tough go there. The bonus is that it also respects privacy, so provided you can keep yourself together, you may have some luck.

Attention getting

This is the most dangerous and destructive kind of affair. You are playing to lose. You care nothing about getting sex, or finding another partner. You want your wife to *notice* that you are having an affair and invest more time and interest in you. To prove you're attractive to another so she'll come back to you.

First, that seems like a good idea to you because you're responsive when she does it. It may only ice her out or make her more distant. Even if it works it has costs. If your basis for an affair is to be blatant, or discovered, to make your partner jealous, consider the first two alternatives below.

Alternatives

So, seriously, is an affair right for you? Don't worry, this isn't a preachy book that promises to tell you how to have an affair, then actually tells you not to. From this section on out we're in "how to" country. That said, having an affair is not for everybody, and you may find it isn't for you, so here are a few alternatives to cheating to think about.

Reconciliation

Now that you've considered why you want to have an affair, ask yourself again *why you want to have an affair.* Maybe the above gave you some insight into paths that you could work on to improve your marriage.

Consider counseling. I know it sounds touchy-feely, but the fact is a good counselor can help you talk through things and give you and your wife permission to rekindle what you've lost. Stay away from "family oriented" or "Christian" counselors.

Here's a hint. The Counselor who agrees with you and puts all the blame on her is not the counselor you want. You can find plenty of conservative counselors to remind wives that in addition to doing the laundry, working a support job, making dinner and minding the children they are also obligated to spread their legs a few times a month.

Accept that you've been part of the problem too and work on actual solutions. That may mean you doing some extra chores in order to make sure that your spouse actually has some energy and feels like a woman for shmexy times. If you don't feel very sexy when you're overworked and taking care of baby barf, how do you expect her to?

A Sex Therapist may be better than a counselor, and many counselors are both. Sex therapists come right in and help put the missing "zing" back in your life. Don't underrate the power of solutions that stick with the woman you...presumably...loved.

Divorce

Maybe you already know you're leaving.

Consider just doing it.

Consider moving ahead with your own life without lining up the next Mrs. Right. As a bachelor, you'll have to adult and take care of yourself, and if failure to do that is part of what led you to the current irrecoverable point you owe it to yourself to man up and learn how not to be a boy in your next relationship. It may be tough and hard but like hitting the gym or buckling down at work, it's the route to manhood.

There are advantages. Especially if there are children, the perception that you left for your own reasons, rather than because of *cheating*, might make relations with your ex less bitter, laying the grounds for an uncontested divorce and easier visitation and custodial arrangements. It may force your ex to focus more on her own contributions to the divorce and take more responsibility rather than focusing on *that tramp* you ran away with, and again, especially if there are children, that may be important in your future happiness.

Polyamory

Monogamy is not the only relationship model out there. Twenty years ago the suggestion that we "see other people" was tantamount to screaming "I don't love you anymore" and just as likely to get a dish thrown at your head. Now with coverage in major Women's magazines and websites, and resources like Franklin Veaux morethantwo.com or Tristan Taormino's openingup.net, there are more resources for people who want to become polyamorous. A recent book by Carrie Jenkins, *What Love Is: And What It Could Be,* has done a lot to drive awareness of "poly" as a lifestyle.

In Polyamory you and your partner see other people. There are far more models than we can go into here. In some cases you see "secondary" partners mostly for sex, in others there may be more commitment up to "Polyfidelity" where you have a closed relationship with only a few other people.

Polyamory is a way of life that works for a lot of people. Is it perfect? No. But if monogamous marriage were perfect, would you be reading this book? It may be a thing to consider for your next "serious" relationship even if it's out of the question for this one.

In practice opening up a marriage works best if part of your reason for cheating is that your partner is already cheating, or emotionally cheating, and the "opening up" is about giving them permission to pursue that.

Be ready for the idea that what's fair for her may not be fair for you. She may be fine with flirting with every man she knows now that you're "open," but constantly denounce your new interests as "beneath you," or "crazy." Be prepared to go slow and do some serious reading to understand how to manage polyamory.

Polyamory works well for men whose motivation is intimacy who need one more person to share their life with.

Sex workers

Many men are inherently revolted at the idea of prostitutes. The terms "dirty" and "diseased" come to mind, complete with drives to some sordid and dangerous part of town where you'll likely get bedbugs and find your car vandalized. Add the criminality in most of the United States with the morbid fear of an arrest record and many men will spend ten thousand dollars on an affair before they will spend three hundred on a professional.

This is the twenty first century.

Sex workers advertise over a variety of social media. Craigslist is no longer the hotbed, and Backpage.com is under assault, however there are many other safe local outlets.

Full instruction in sex work is outside the scope of our book, but here's a good start. Join theeroticreview.com. Not only will you find well reviewed providers but discussion boards that give invaluable information.

Doubtless some of the people on those boards are cops. But the vast majority aren't. Go by the numbers as you would for buying goods of Amazon. A girl with ten good reviews, by ten members who have been around for five years and written hundreds of reviews is not a cop.

TER as it is known will provide you with an excellent "newbies" section where you can learn about meeting providers. You may also learn about "referral" services which will, for a fee, verify your employment and identity. Read up on these services in the forums. Hint...the ones that

Joseph Sebstian

are referenced in many provider's profiles/websites as being accepted are the ones that are legit.

Many men consider the cost dissuasive. A good, clean, encounter in which you will absolutely receive oral and be allowed penetration by an attractive woman who has no reservations about initiating sex with you will run between $200 and 600, assuming your idea of "attractive" is "prettier and younger than your wife," and not "a porn star." Porn star dates and Girlfriend Experience (GFE) in which the girl goes on a date with you and talks, will run $1200 and up. That may sound like a lot, but if you start adding up all the expenses of conducting an affair you will quickly find it's a bargain. We'll get to the economics of affairs later.

A quote, possibly apocryphal, attributed to Ernest Hemingway, was that "Some men pay whores to be with them. Others pay whores so they will go home afterwards." Sex workers are the ultimate uncomplicated affair.

Other types of sex work

Obviously prostitution works better if your need is primarily sexual. You may even find it fires up your home sex life. If your need is emotional there are other types of sex workers. Phone sex operators, video chat operators, and some text operators may provide more in the way of actual companionship. If you need companionship or the pretense of a relationship, you may want to look primarily at GFE providers, particularly those who get strong marks in this area.

17

If your issue is wanting to be Kinky, especially wanting to be submissive, when your wife does not want to be dominant, you may want to look into a professional dominatrix. This can be attractive because prodomme services which do not include sex are typically legal, or at least quasi-legal. That said, many girls on TER are "kink friendly" usually meaning they'll dominate you, not let you dominate them.

A minor sidetrack on social politics

You're a gentleman. You don't call them whores and they don't call you...oh man who is about to cheat..."filthy cheating trash." The era launched by Playboy in 1949 is one in which gentlemen promote sexual tolerance, rather than shitting on it. Don't like "liberated women?" Just who, exactly, are you hoping to have an affair with. A closely kept housewife who got married at 18 and stays at home? Unless your day job is "plumber," women's liberation is the side your bread is buttered on.

Think you hate all feminists? You probably don't. If you identify feminism with shutting men down, being negative towards sex and generally sucking the fun out of life, you probably hate "sex negative feminists." Look around for "sex positive feminists." That's where fun and the cosmopolitan modern world lie.

Summary

If you aren't already caught up in an affair and trying desperately to pull it off, perhaps you have a better idea what you are looking for. That's good because it's going to determine the kind of girl you go after.

Note we're presuming you're interested in a woman. We don't deal explicitly with LGBT affairs here, but if you're in a straight marriage but want a male partner, many of the tips here will work for you, though the psychology of your partner may be different. If you're in a male-male marriage, the history of cruising and anonymous sex in gay history may make for a very different proposition, leaving you with a partner who may be far more canny about what it is you are trying to do, but also potentially more understanding about your need to do it.

Our strongest commandment is Know Thyself. Later in this book we'll present a checklist to allow you to figure out whether or not you are "ready" for an affair.

Know the Objective

An amazing number of men understand, literally, nothing about women. We're going to present a very rough guide. It's based on science but it's designed for the lay reader, or rather the leader who wants to get laid. It deals in generalities and many people today might find it offensive, but like a Cosmo article on "what men want" it's just designed to hit the statistical high points. We'll also note that the science here is biased towards people who bought this book and the people they are likely to meet looking in the places people find partners to cheat with. We focus on norms for the roughly half the human race that's disposed to cheat and does.

We already know what kind of girl you want to have an affair with. She's young, a circus freak in the bedroom, infinitely into you, infinitely patient, and understands the pre-emptive importance of your marriage. She is soft spoken and does what you ask and she would never, never, never cause you problems in your life. When you're not around she's self sufficient, she has her own, clean, place, and she doesn't need expensive dates or gifts, she just wants you.

The science

The science of babymaking for people who don't want babies

We're going to talk a lot here about "reproductive strategy" and babies. We know that you're probably not interested in having a baby (in fact we'll talk more about that under

"dangers") and your partner probably isn't either.
Consciously.

But it isn't your cold conscious mind that's driving you to
cheat is it? You didn't sit down and make a list of possible
entertainments and projects and list "clean garage, fix toilet,
have sexual intercourse with someone other than my wife."
It wasn't a logical process.

That's because when it comes to sex, we're driven by our
subconscious mind and often we're just along for the ride.
The more we understand about our drives…and those of the
people we want to have sex with, the more happy and
successful we'll be.

So, you may just want to get off, or do that freaky thing from
that porn video. But somewhere deep down in your brain,
your instincts want to gather young fertile partners to pump
sperm into, so that they will bear children who perpetuate
your genes.

There isn't room to explain how natural/sexual selection
works here, but the short version is that we instinctively
behave like the animals that had the best behaviors for
keeping themselves alive and producing offspring, because
those are the animals that passed their genes along. When we
talk about "sexual strategies," that's the culmination of
millions of years of instinct.

What do men want?

Remember we talked about how biology says you're driven to
spread your seed around, to try and father children. Well

women may be out for the "O" or "fun" but in their subconscious mind they're out to have something that isn't very fun and starts with a "b."

The drive isn't as simple as yours though. If you impregnate a woman, she is going to fight to keep that offspring alive. She'll recruit any man she can to keep that baby alive, and offer him whatever favors she needs to. Even if you walk away and you never see her again there's a chance that he'll live to adulthood. And because some distant ancestor of yours did that, the strategy is still with you.

Of course your children have a better chance of living to adulthood if you stick around to take care of them. Which is why we have the pair bonding instincts that led you to the altar, at least if you went willingly. But trying to spread your seed as wide as possible adds chances at no great cost to you. So, sure you'll have sex anytime you can without chance of ruining your marriage or health.

What do women want?

It's a different deal for her. Once she's pregnant, she is in danger. She is going to slow down and be clumsier, less able to gather food (remember our deep genetic instincts don't really get pizza delivery), and more in need of protection. What's the worst case scenario? To be abandoned, without anyone to feed her, or care for her while she's giving birth. That's a death sentence.

Throughout history women who are pregnant have survived better (remember that means passed along their instincts) if they had powerful men around them to fend off predators.

Having other, nurturing, women probably helps too, but that's outside of your control.

By instinct, sex is a package deal for women. They want the man, not just the sperm. So if this is true, why do women ever cheat?

Most women cheat for the same reason men do. They feel trapped, unsexy, need to prove they still have it...everything we wrote about above. If they already have a husband they may not feel so threatened that cheating feels like a tremendous risk.

That said, their biology does drive what traits they are attracted to. And many men undersell themselves on easy wins because they don't understand this. Later we're going to talk about ways to improve yourself to be "what women want."

We're not talking about some namby pamby socially correct ideal, or princess mentality. We will tell you what women want of men that they are going to have sex with on the side and that is driven by millions of years of evolution. You can complain, you can post rants, but you can't change nature. The only thing you can do is make it work in your favor.

Two types of men

Studies by Dr. Stephanie Gangestad and others have strongly suggested that women are more likely to "hook up" with attractive strangers when they are ovulating, and have a stronger preference for men with strong physical features that are known to indicate high testosterone, including a "masculine" chin and harder facial features. This tendency has been proven over a number of studies, and despite recent attempts to refute it by people who don't like the idea, it has borne out in studies more often than not.

Other researchers have suggested this leads to a pattern in women. They prefer to pair bond with a moderately attractive but more "maternal" male who will be more invested in raising children. The less masculine male will trade child care and fidelity for occasional sexual access, and a chance of siring offspring.

Sperm roulette

However women instinctively want to the best sperm they can, and that may not come from their more maternal long term partner. So they may be drawn to cheat with attractive and more masculine strangers when they are ovulating. Women may not know consciously what is driving them or that they are ovulating, but it doesn't change the "seeking" behaviors, or the openness to an encounter they might otherwise reject.

What does this mean?

It means that five hundred thousand whiny men on OKStupid! and in dozens of other apps are doing it wrong. They beg for sex, or talk about how their wife doesn't want them anymore in an apparent attempt to get sympathy. Alternatively they may be mindlessly pushy, because that worked once, and not understand why it seldom works a second time.

You need to know the type of affair you want to have. Do you want a sizzling few times a month pairing with a single or married woman? Or do you want an intimate bedroom exchange where you get to act out your fantasies of how your life could have been and play house.

If you want the sort of affair we most often picture, little fuss, little muss, a girl who wants quiet secret sex with you and then wants to go away, you're looking for a stable woman with a slightly effeminate partner. Your job is to be more exciting, dangerous, and interesting than her current partner or partners. She isn't inclined to leave him because he's the maternal man who will raise her children (even if her only actual ward is a Pomeranian).

If you want an affair which is more nurturing and emotional, you may be looking to play the more stable and maternal partner to a younger girl, who is willing to accept the idea you're not "full time" because you offer so much stability. The stability can be largely emotional and perceptual. You have the advantage that just as the girl is not thinking "I want him to father my child and take care of it," she may respond emotionally to cues that you are prosperous, stable, and caring, without needing a lot of actual financial investment. Understanding what she wants can help you paint this picture. Smiling at babies and always picking up the tab at dinner without a production, being calm and never complaining about money or bad treatment, being polite to waitstaff can send a message that you are that stable, slightly maternal, man in her life.

How to get the woman you don't want

There are a lot of resources that can tell you more about getting the woman you want, including our upcoming book *The Art and Science of Hook Ups*. For now, we'll stick to generalities specific to affairs.

It's proven science that both men and women tend to approach potential partners who are more attractive than they are, and settle for partners who, rated by impartial observers, are about as attractive.

Married men usually end up with slightly less attractive partners in an affair, because attractiveness is an overall package. For women, youth and physical beauty play a large part. For men strong testosterone sculpted features can matter, but so do wealth and power.

The more desperate you are the more desperate they will be

When men imagine that women think like they do, they make mistakes. Let's look at desperation. If you met a pretty young girl, struggling in college, who was desperate for your time and attention, would you sleep with her? Absent other reasons not to, probably. In fact you might even do it if she weren't so pretty if she seemed really easy to get into the sack.

So, many men who are looking for affairs present themselves pathetically. They wheedle, talk about how miserable they are in comparison to their previous relationship. They may say that their wife ices them out or cheats on them.

Let's frame this out.

You say "my wife cheats on me all the time."
She hears "my own wife doesn't want my sperm anymore,"
and she thinks "why the hell would I?"

You say "I'm bored and miserable," she hears "I'm boring
and miserable."

So who do you get? Well, imagine a girl desperate enough
that sleeping with a man your wife won't seems like a good
idea. Do you think she's a lot of fun? Is fun in bed? If so
why isn't she dating someone else?

The woman who wants you despite your failings has plans for you

So despite all this you find a woman who is falling over
herself to date you. She's attractive, has some social status,
seems to think a lot of herself. She's invested in you. And
she really truly doesn't matter that you're married. She's
happy to keep your secrets.

You're not super attractive. But she doesn't care. She says
you'll "clean up well." She's responding to you just like you
were the maternal guy who was going to be her baby daddy
but you're not.

...that's what you think.

We're not saying that she's going to end up boiling your
daughter's rabbit, but she does have designs. You're the next

Mr. Right. Maybe she'll let it drift along and hope you just run your marriage down out of attrition. Or maybe she has plans to *help*.

Now, we've talked about the unconscious mind. We're not saying this girl is actively plotting to undo your marriage. But her unconscious mind? People are very good at planning things in their unconscious mind and not admitting them to themselves.

Women aren't secret agents

Anne Desclos, the actual name of the woman who wrote the classic novel *Story of O*, a half century before *Fifty Shades of Grey* came along, was a member of the French Resistance during the Nazi occupation. She worked with famed writer Jean Paulhan. They conducted a very secret affair for over thirty years using dead drops, payphones, and secret meeting places, just as they had during Resistance Days.

Anne Desclos was devoted to Paulhan, had some pretty interesting sexual interests, and happened to be a secret agent. She also lived in a culture where secret affairs were a standard, and important men were expected to keep a mistress. She might be the ideal affair, but you probably won't find a secret agent in modern America.

Just like a few men get off on the secrecy of illicit relationships, the power of controlling people around them, so do some women. They conduct affairs, keep them compartmentalized, and have no interest in anyone finding out.

28

They're rare, and if they're at all attractive they can look for very high value partners. They may have a chain of lovers who are leaders in a community. And even then they may not be able to avoid having a little fun playing them off or yanking the chains.

Women aren't secret agents. They aren't going to instinctively keep your secrets while giving you all the pleasure in the world. Don't expect a secret agent.

Women aren't crazy, but the ones you meet may be

There are a lot of memes out there along the lines of "men are dumb, women are crazy." This translates as "men are emotionally tone deaf, women are emotionally erratic." To some extent this is true. Research has shown that women are more empathetic than men, where empathy is defined as being able to read social cues, understand social context, and react to signs of others social distress.

Women's behavior may also be affected by hormones, causing subtle or major shifts in behavior over a month. In general women who don't experience major shifts end to disbelieve those who experience them, and those who do experience them can go years believing that they are simply "train wrecks" or "a hot mess" rather than experiencing hormonal surges. Part of the problem is that whatever behavior we are engaging in at the moment feels normal to us, even if we later realize it was out of line.

Men may also tend to believe women are crazy because they move based on urges we don't see or understand. A man who sneaks out to meet a lover isn't seen as "crazy" but "scheming" or "mean." A man who compulsively confesses his cheating is seen as "weak" or even "honest." Similar driven behaviors in women are more mysterious because we don't get the reason. A woman who rounds savagely on a lover may be cutting off the fling who she wanted briefly, in order to keep safe her position with the more maternal man she is hoping to raise her children. A woman who berates her "kind" husband may be trying to cow him into submission in order to have more latitude to seek masculine partners for secret liaisons. The game of being cruel to our partner in order to beat them into acceptance of our own straying is played by all genders.

Behavior isn't "crazy" just because you don't understand the motivations. If you think about the drives and issues we've outlined here, there is usually some sort of pattern. When you add all the motives we reviewed above, women who appear "crazy" are usually acting in support of one of those motives, or in a panic reaction because they were driven to "go too far" and need to step back to feel safe.

That said, you may tend to meet more emotionally unstable women. Being in a relationship is safe, and even if half of us cheat, we're not all doing it at one time. Women who decide to cheat right now are usually experiencing emotional upheaval or distress, or strongly driven by sexual urges. None of those make for "typical" behavior. Knowing what is driving the women you meet will help you to understand and manage reactions.

Women have emotional needs

We started by saying that women are not secret agents who exist for your sexual needs. We've already talked about the importance of recognizing why you want to cheat. We want to close by emphasizing that you should make every effort to determine why your partner is cheating.

Whether you want a one-time hookup, or a long-running affair, cheating can be emotionally tough and sap energy. Having it go smoothly makes that easier. Unhappy partners can also create real dangers.

Too many men ignore their own motives, allow themselves to be driven to an affair primarily by sex urge, just want to "get it in" and assume the same thing is driving their partner. They're surprised when things blow up.

Try to get a sense of her needs. You can't trust her exact words, though women are more likely to have analyzed their reasons for an affair (outside of the masculine stranger thing) more carefully than men. Look for underlying patterns. Does she need to feel more valued, safer, more desirable.

Provide that. It costs you very little, and will make your own life far smoother and less stressful.

The Rules

Ready? Here are the core rules you need to live by if you are going to do this thing

Don't get caught

No seriously. Even if you decide at some point that you wish to reveal your affair...and we don't think that's ever very wise...you want to do it on your own terms. You need to commit to doing the things, before and after, that will ensure that you do not get caught.

Don't confess

A widely reported 2016 survey by IllicitEncounters.com found that women were less likely than men to forgive cheating. The reason? Men are more likely to believe their partner cheated because they weren't given enough attention, while Women assume cheating is a deep-rooted instinct which will happen again and again. With a few exceptions they're right. Women are also much better and keeping their affair concealed so...we're going to build your "A" game.

Your lover is a person

If you want to have sex with a girl you need to understand she's a person too. First it's human decency. But even if you are the ultimate callous lover, with no regard for others, it's a basic matter of smooth sailing and survival. Ultimately it may be a matter of of even having an affair, since men who can't recognize women as people find it hard to get a desirable woman into bed.

Don't confuse this with saying you have to be politically correct or behave a certain way. Many women want a demanding, strong-willed man to exert control and tell them what to do.

If you do not want endless complications in your life, you will start with regard for your lover as a person and recognize that if you want something so do they. Figure out what it is and provide it, or if you can't, apologize and move on.

Presenting Yourself

If you're George Clooney and have no problem getting girls, go ahead and skip this section. But if you've wondered why they just don't seem as keen as they used to, or...why they never seemed as keen for you as some of your friends, it's time to start developing your "A" game, by starting with yourself.

You're going back into dating. Only you're not just dating. You're dating with a giant chain around your waist. It's a handicap, and if you are going to offset it, you don't just need to bring the same game you brought when single. You need to bring a much, much, better game. Hopefully age, treachery, and experience will get you far, but you need every advantage you can get.

What if it's not a date?

What if you aren't actually dating. You're chatting online, or trying to pick a girl up through a night class on art history? How does that work? Generally, the same. If it is a date to *you*, dress for it and act like it. If it's online, apply all the conversational rules below.

Many women won't date a married man on their way to having sex with him. It's important to them that they feel they "just fell" into the affair (remember that thing we warned you not to do) so there are shared activities, increasing intimacy, and finally some setup to get alone and have sex. You need to identify these things, and skew them in your favor without being so obvious it sets off alarm bells.

The woman who behaves like this is not just cheating on her husband. One part of her mind is cheating on the part that tries to make her behave, and you need to help her keep it on the downlow until the thing has happened. Even then, calling it an affair might be dangerous. Just making it "our thing" may be the best path. Many good affairs have happened like this. Occasional lovers who met through a hobby, have sex, but otherwise simply behave as friends. With the right two people it can be a good, low maintenance, outlet. Often they see it as part of the activity. "I don't cheat on my marriage, but when I go to our quarterly conference, I sleep with Zach." The sex is a benefit of the "festival friendship," not an "affair," which would place it as a challenge to the marriage.

That said, we like affairs where both parties have eyes open rather than affairs where one party is fooling themselves. It becomes easy to decide that the affair was "not what I meant to do," and even engage in revenge based on having been "coerced" into sex.

Appearance and grooming

Time to take it to a mirror. Just how do you look? It's time to seriously consider what damage a few years of marriage has done to you, since the days when you used to have to clean up to go on a date.

Because you did do that, right?

If you didn't you're going to have to start. Being a softball shirt wearing slob in High School may have still gotten you a girl, but dressing like a refugee from a teen heartthrob show is probably not going to work so well for you now. Unless you actually are under 25, buy some grown up clothes and look decent.

This isn't a random tip. Back then you were appealing to a girl who wanted her first man, ideally a combination of maternal and masculine, but at least one or the other. She wanted a boy to be with. Now she's been around once or twice and she's looking for a man. You'd better be a man. Occasional 80s songs aside, very few women are on the prowl for men younger than themselves, especially men emotionally younger than themselves.

So. Shave. Get your hair styled. Go to a stylist of the sort who charges more than $50 for a haircut and take their advice on what to do with your hair. Get clothes that make you look like you're a grownup.

Cologne

Cologne can be a friend but don't overdo it. You can overwhelm your own natural musk. Also don't overdo deodorants unless you're planning to do a lot of physical activity. Your sweat conveys pheromones which may ignite sexual interest. That's why dance clubs get sexed up...people sweat through their clothes. Use a deodorant under the armpits only and avoid kid products like Axe.

Look online for rankings of how sexy women find colognes. What do you care how it smells? You want her to like it. Invest in something that's over $30 for best effect. You can buy anything online these days, so don't skimp. The best ranked in the world is Yves Saint Laurent La Nuit De L'homme, but you might want something more exotic like Viktor & Rolf Spicebomb Eau De Toilette Spray for Men. Old fallbacks like Paco Rabanne and Polo Black aren't bad choices, just remember that the "as good as" imitations sold in convenience stores aren't fit to be poured down the toilet. We know *you* can't smell the difference. The parts of those colognes that make them worth $70 hit the hindbrain, not the forebrain.

You might want to give yourself a little advantage by using a cologne that includes pheromones. The note here is that women who are into you or into sex right now will think it smells great, but it may drive others away. If you do this, use a name brand. Most off-brand concoctions are, at the least unhelpful. Pheromone for men by Marilyn Miglin is probably your safest bet. Liquid Trust Pheromone spray comes with reasonable reviews and may be more helpful than a sex attractant. It is designed to help build trust, which may be more important than passion in getting a girl to go to bed with a stranger or married man.

The cover: Your partner may notice that you've suddenly upped your game, and that's one way that men make it very obvious that they're having an affair. Try and frame your change in terms of some job opportunity. "Bob said if I wanted to be considered for management school I needed to look better in meetings," or "I read an article that if you dressed to succeed you could increase your salary by 20% over four years." Make sure there is no specific, provable, objective. You may want to let your wife dress you and play consultant. If she has input and buy in to your new "look" she may be happy to see you go out of the house dressed for a date.

Don't bring her into the cologne picture, she won't make a good pick for you. A good way to introduce a new cologne is to start wearing a tiny bit at a time. Have it arrive as a "gift from mom" and if she says she hates it, occasionally "forget" before going back to your usual, so it's not too alarming if you smell different. For suspicious products like Pheromone, consider buying a cheaper (glass) bottle, preferably of an alcohol based scent that can be more easily cleaned out. Wash the bottle for about ten minutes in hot water, with soap. Then wash it again. Then decant your secret scent into the more prosaic bottle and...you can keep it in your medicine cabinet alongside that aging can of Axe body spray.

Culture

All through this book we're going to be talking about norms. That varies from culture to culture. If you live in Bethlehem PA, and nobody you know wears a suit, then "adult clothes" doesn't mean a suit. It does mean not dressing like a kid. The object is to stand out, a little, from the crowd around you. Be just a little better dressed. Women notice that and it gives you automatic high status. Where it's not acceptable to dress "differently" at all, then have better hair and personal grooming. The idea isn't to be a fish out of water, but to be subtly better than everyone around you so that you are identified as the "high value" man to win.

We focus a lot on middle class Americans and British, because they're the people who have the social mobility to have affairs. If "a nice suit" isn't what you'd wear, figure out the equivalent in your own culture whether it's rattlesnake boots or Bally sneakers.

No idea what you should wear, and afraid your wife is dressing you funny? GQ has an online edition that can be of some help. Get an idea of what popular "looks" are and start taking notice of the best dressed men around you.

Conversation

We didn't talk much about intelligence in our discussion of what women seek in men. A major online site asked Martie Haselton, a UCLA psychologist, about the importance of intelligence. "The take-home message...is that intelligence is probably always pretty important for a woman...low intelligence is not really a turn-on for anybody."

Yeah that. This explains a great deal about most online dating services. Smart men already have dates, so many of the profiles are put up by non-smart men.

You don't have to be Will Hunting to get girls interested, but you absolutely, positively have to be interesting.

Six tips:

Know the situation

Know something about the place you are, or the situation. If you're meeting after a night film school class, know something about film. If you're taking her to a trendy

downtown restaurant, know something about the chef. If
you had a chance to read up on her interests from a profile,
try to know something about them, but don't *ever* try to
impress her that you know more about her interests than she
does. Many men try and use these bits of knowledge to
overwhelm a woman and establish clear superiority. You may
do that so well that she doesn't want to come back. It's a
give and take. Throw out your bits of information as
amusing notes like in a film, not as a college lecture.

Have some anecdotes

Have a few amusing stories about things that have happened
to you. If they are true so much the better, but friend's funny
experiences are good too. Here's the rule. If you end up
looking like a champ in the end, the middle part needs to
have you on the ropes. "I had no idea how to ski...I mean I
was scared to death, I gotta tell you...but then there I was
crossing the line!" If you fail that can be cute and disarming,
but you need to tie it together with a life lesson so you don't
seem lame. "I ended up in a huge pile and was in a cast for a
week...since then I learned when the instructor says go, you
better go!" Admitting emotions in the moment, such as fear,
while discussing them calmly and competently, can make you
seem very together and in control.

No drama

Seriously, none. Do not share that your mother recently died
of cancer. Do not share your misgivings about your wife.
Do not share your own personal angst. Women want men
who are masculine (thus unemotional and in control) or
competently maternal (which does not involve losing your
shit). "I like having a man be emo at me on a first date," said

no. Woman. Ever. None. Are there ways to salvage it? Sure. Can it play into building rapport? Sure. But it is never going to be a good thing. If you discuss things like your mother dying, or your wife's infidelity, be cheery and resigned. "Well things like that happen...it's a tragedy of course, but there's not much point in getting bogged down in it."

There are constructive ways to show your sensitive side. Being dramatic about your own life is not one of them.

Don't mansplain

This term has gotten so widely stretched to mean any time a man explains anything that the original meaning has been lost. That said, understand this: (a) it is a thing women actually hate, that's why they made up a name for it and (b) because it's discussed a lot today, women are hyper aware when a man is doing it.

Mansplaining is basically to be patronizing usually when explaining something unnecessary or that the woman already knows. Usually at length.

Wrong:
She: I loved Titanic. Did you know that James Cameron actually dove down to the wreck?
He: Begins a 20 minute explanation of Cameron's diving career, including details of his Challenger Deep descent

Right:
She: I loved Titanic. Did you know that James Cameron actually dove down to the wreck?

He: Yeah. Did you know he's dived to the Challenger Deep and fewer humans have been there than have gone to the moon? I thought that was incredible. How did you learn about the Titanic thing?

Maybe she asks what the Challenger Deep is, and you tell her. Maybe she tells you she's actually a Marine Biologist who did graduate work at Woods Hole and you don't end up looking like an idiot. You move on, a sentence or two at a time, never more than a short paragraph. Try to ask questions as well as supplying answers.

Note "I thought that was incredible." You're not lecturing her on facts you know. You're conveying passion for something.

You may manage to overwhelm her with your complete superiority. So much so that she realizes she'll never be anything serious to you and decides to go for a younger man who she can be more of an equal to. Don't overdo it.

Some women *like* the man to lecture and lead. If she seems to naturally fall into this, you can loosen up a bit, but watch for smiles and body language indicating she's actually interested. Also don't be offended if she doesn't remember anything you said. Odds are she's taking the opportunity to analyze how you talk, and unconsciously assess the shape of your face, your clothing and all the other markers that tell her whether or not you're worthwhile.

Keep your situation to soundbites

The surest way to advertise your failings is to talk at length about your marriage and its problems. On the other hand, if it's clear you're married, you have to say *something*.

Remember that on some level the girl is going to be comparing herself to your wife. If she really wants you, she may be able to label your wife a "bitch" in her mind, and feel no sympathy for her. But on another level she's thinking "will I end up like that?"

Talking about your wife is a lose/lose. If she's so into you that she is on board with it and doesn't care, you waste valuable time where you could be engaging her and building rapport. If she's not that into you, it's not going to convince her to take the plunge and may even drive her to pulling the plug. It's venting for you that doesn't get you what you want. If what you really want is just for someone to listen to you gripe about your wife, find a friend or a counselor.

So what do you say? Have some soundbites. The first level can sound breezy.

"Well, I try to do my best but we don't seem to get along anymore."

Once you've thrown those out, have a level of more human and emotional soundbites ready. Encapsulate each problem in a mature, emotional, thought. Don't be afraid to run yourself down a little. It makes you seem more honest.

Gentleman's Guide to Cheating

"I made some mistakes with her emotionally. I didn't listen when she needed me to, and now we're not close anymore. I wish it weren't that way, but I can't turn time back, and I can't spend the next ten years trying to make up for those things."

Don't put the "D" word on the table unless she addresses it. If she does, up the ante.

"Look I really like you. But I've got to be honest. I don't know that divorce is going to happen. I'd like to be with you and spend time together, but you know my situation and you're an adult. I don't want to string you along thinking I'm offering to get divorced. I'm not that kind of man."

In the end, you'll do better if you are honest on this point. We'll talk more about when, and how you should be honest about your marriage and life in general, but if it's clear you're a married man, you need to be clear about expectations if you don't want dangerous scenes later on.

Listen

Women want to talk about themselves, and the date you're on. Try just listening. The strong silent type can be sexy.

Know what women like to talk about:

Her life, self, the date, and you

What she likes and dislikes, how she is with her family, where she went to school, what her parents are like, what her hopes and dreams are.

44

Travel places, and food

Talking about places you've been, far and near is always good. Try to plan your dialog, and make it interesting. A short, emotional, statement on the impact of Angkor Wat is a lot better than an hour long travelog. Have anecdotes that are breezy and funny. Remember the rule...if you end up looking brilliant you have to have a moment of actual stress, confusion or danger. "So at that point I was scared witless. I had no idea where the taxi driver was taking us..." If you end up looking foolish, end with a moral that redeems you. "I realized these people really don't have the advantages we do."

Be very careful making up stories about places you haven't actually been. It may come up that she knows a few obvious details that you don't. "You know...the big observation wheel in London? You've *seen* it at least!"

Remember that places close to home can be just as exciting if the stories are good. Interesting restaurants, out of the way shopping places, or artisanal towns in the region can be great things to share, and they suggest possible future getaways.

Pets

Pets are a great icebreaker. One reason is that pets are a way of assessing if you have any maternal instincts. If you're going for the quick chisel-chinned seduction, you may want to disclaim an interest in pets, but if you want any sort of a relationship a little cooing over dogs and cats can be good. Show an interest in hers, and tell a few stories about yours, past or current. Going into detail about your current pets can be a way to make her feel she knows more about you.

Shared hobbies

If she has a genuine interest in a hobby you share, great. If you met at a ballgame, talk about the team. If you like a certain kind of music, go to town. Here, even more than above, it's important to remember to exchange information, not to hammer her with it. If it's a shared interest and she feels pounded, rather than a fun point of connection, it can become a point of frustration.

If it isn't a *shared* hobby, let it rest, even if she asks about it. If she says "oh I've always wanted to learn to play poker," do not regale her with twenty minutes of the World Series of Poker. One breezy story or a throwaway line is enough "you'd be good at it, you've got a good smile and I don't always know what you're thinking." If it's a major attractant like the fact you BASE jump, or do motor racing, focus on telling her about the thrill and emotion of it, not the boring details. Describing a sports hobby can conjure up images of what you'd be like in bed or the whole affair.

Wrong: "when you're taking turns fast, the most important thing is your tires. You need to keep track of how sticky or tacky the track is, and how much rubber you've burned...you need to adhere to the track."

Right: "fast turns are exciting. You're pumping into them, and you can't hold on too tight. You have to trust your instincts and hold the car gently, letting it drift, then slowly pull it back into place...it's almost like falling, dangerous and exhilarating..."

The first is technically accurate. The second is a metaphor for sex and your relationship.

For shared hobbies, movies or media is usually a good fallback. Be careful not to latch onto the one series you've seen in common particularly if it's geeky or 'guy-centric.' Move around, and encourage her to talk about media she likes, even if you aren't as familiar with it.

Share things you don't like

This is a little tricky. Shared hates can actually be a very powerful bonding tool. Try asking her "so what things drive you the most crazy," and find common ground. Maybe you both hate pretentious people, or bad service, or religious crazies. The rule? Keep your passion one notch below hers. She needs to see you as a co-conspirator in fun, not the next Charles Manson with a dangerous rant just below the surface. If she starts getting too impassioned, back off to another topic, but not before validating that you can see her point. She'll usually calm down within a few moments and feel embarrassed, happy you let her off the hook. If she doesn't, depending on what and why she was so upset, you may want to consider that this is not the person you want to have an affair with.

Share secrets

Shared secrets are a powerful way to create a bond. The problem is that knowing what kind of secrets to share is often difficult, and the line between "bonding" and "oversharing," can be a razor's edge.

Be careful what you say to strangers. One plus is that your casual secrets don't have to be true, just emotionally impactful. It's all about framing here.

"When I was 12, I killed a rabbit with my dad's 22 rifle" can be a tender coming of age story that demonstrates pain and compassion, or it can be the first telltale sign that she's going to end up putting the lotion in the basket. If you aren't sure of the reception, leave well enough alone.

If you actually have a lot of awful secrets, consider a counselor, not a random first date. You may in fact have seen a man's head blown 200 yards by an IED, or seen medics cut the struggling fetus from a dead and mangled Iraqi woman, but bringing your PTSD to dinner paints you as a likely sea of problems. Some women are really curious about death, pain, torture and it's okay to hint, and then follow up if she asks, but float a terrible detail at a time, and make sure that you convey the emotional impact, even if it's by saying "it's hard to explain how you feel about these things. After a while you talk about them very calmly but they sink down into your mind and make you uneasy."

Again, don't exaggerate. Turning your Call of Duty games into a tour of duty in Mosul may seem brilliant on a first date, but there are many bad real-world consequences for that sort of lying, and the odds you'll eventually be made an ass of, at the last, are high. Getting fed your teeth by an actual Marine when your drunk date tells him that *you* actually disarmed an IED is probably the best case scenario.

Men we know have had surprising success with disclosing sexual secrets. A risque affair on a vacation, or with a colleague. Women are strangely fascinated by prostitution, and talking about your date with a high priced callgirl can be fascinating. The advantage to these is that you can use them to frame out your sexual expectations for the affair. Use some sense here. Some women are curious others are intensely jealous. If she clearly doesn't even like the thought you've slept with other women, this is baiting, not sharing secrets. Don't do it.

Manners

Whatever your social group, have the best manners possible. Don't be ridiculous or bizarre. If people in your culture make women get into the pickup truck themselves and honk out front, then do that.

That said, most Americans who are likely to be reading this book are at least somewhat involved in the mainstream media and television driven culture which values things like opening doors and not eating like swine.

The website **artofmanliness.com** offers realistic modern information on manners designed for real people in day to day life. Brooks Brothers, the clothing company, publishes a book called *How to be a Gentleman* by John Bridges. It's short and very readable.

Common fail points with manners

The car

With remotes it's increasingly common to simply unlock the door, rather than helping a woman into the car. Watch for her cues and consider escorting her if there's any issue. Being overly solicitous about the car can leave you looking like you are trying too hard.

Doors

Don't batter your way through a door and let it slam in her face. It's still polite to open doors. If it's a double door she may open the inner door for you. Take it and let her pass in front of you, or if her body language indicates you should go through before her, just do that. Be smooth and don't fight.

Phones

Leave your phone alone, even if she doesn't leave hers alone. You're the strong one, remember. If you need to actually check mail, or show her something give a perfunctory apology. This also serves as a hint that spending most of your date gabbing on Facebook with her friend is not welcome.

That said, many women play games on their phones as something to do with their hands, in the same way people in previous generations smoked. It's not necessarily an insult if she fiddles with the phone while talking to you. Making a 'deal' out of it may be counterproductive. If you're an older man trying to date younger women, be respectful of their phone use. It's going to seem odd to you, but it's just part of the way the world works now.

Restaurant staff and tips

How you treat service personnel provides her a lot of information about how secure a human being you are. If you behave like a spoiled child, complaining, privately or out loud, if you undertip, you'll seem like an ass, and she may decide you aren't worth the trouble. Treat any service staff politely and decently even if they absolutely do not deserve it. Tip 20% without undue attention.

Don't check the bill

When the bill comes, put your card in the folder with a perfunctory glance and when it is returned, do the quickest possible math to get 20% and write in the tip, if it isn't already calculated or handled through a payment station.

Hint. Take a zero off the end of the total, and then double it, rounding as you go.
$89.20 = $8.90 = $18.00 - you might even consider rounding that to $20. Wildly overtipping is gauche, but rounding to a larger bill is fine.

Scrutinizing the bill is a big issue. If she's already squirming that you are the one paying (and many women feel very conflicted about that) having you looking like you've just lost your firstborn child when the bill comes may be a big emotional blow to her that undoes the good of a posh evening out.

Sexual consent

Consent is a huge topic in the younger world right now. To many men it may seem poisonous with horror stories of college campuses where every action must be preceded by a question…"May I kiss you?"

Putting your head in the sand like an ostrich may put you off limits for younger girls, or even end up with a rape charge floating to your doorstep.

Outside of college campuses, a lot of sexual interaction is unspoken. She gets a look in her eyes, there is slight movement, you kiss. Later, you're both excited. Your hand goes to the back of her head and you unzip…she puts her lips around you. Later still you slide into her, after putting on a condom or not. We'll talk later about birth control and condoms.

You need to be aware of the current social dialog on consent, particularly with younger and better educated women.

We don't recommend that you ask "would you like to…" at every step. We do recommend that you get verbal consent for anything beyond kissing, unless there is clear, abundant, physical consent. If she's tearing at your zipper you don't need to ask her questions. But if you're the one instigating, you should be the one asking.

It doesn't have to be unromantic. Restraint in a man can be sexy, even a tease. Rising from a passionate kiss, putting your hand on the top button of your shirt and saying "do you want to do this?" can be effective without seeming like you're a blushing sophomore. Questions like "are you sure you want this?" or "is this what you want?" whispered in a husky voice make sure she's on board with what is going on.

You don't want to discover later that she was in some different place, where you believed you were enthusiastically moving forward, and she believed she was trapped with a commanding older man who was making demands of her.

The more enthusiasm you can get from her, the better. If you feel you are having to push her to sex, consider calling it a night. She'll either try harder next time, or you'll get a no next time which means it was *never* a good idea.

Never beg, except playfully. Some girls may like to tease in the moment and a bit of that is fine if it doesn't bother you. But having to beg her for access to her body is a bad place to start and unless you have a kink that drives you in that direction, you are never going to be completely safe or happy with that relationship.

Be Valuable

By the standards of your community, communicate solid prospects and wealth. Understand by wealth we don't mean, exactly, that you have a lot of money. Casually carding a meal without checking the receipt, or calling Uber Black instead of an economy car, says a lot more about your actual wealth than talking about your investments or pay scale.

Remember, to her, your wealth and social status is about as important as her looks are to you. Not because she's greedy or mean, but because on a subconscious level, that tells her how likely you are to be able to support offspring. And the ante goes up if she knows you're already supporting another woman's children.

Wait a minute. How do things like wealth matter?

Money is a human social construct. How does an unconscious that's concerned with making babies and surviving the winter care about an Uber Black car?

We are trying to tap into the instinctual gut responds to the idea of power in a man. Our subconscious mind doesn't understand Uber, but it has been trained since birth to know that certain types of clothes, vehicles, or ways of speaking indicate status and power.

The important thing to know is that women aren't like you. If a girl is pretty, even if she's poor or badly educated, you may want her. If you're handsome, that might get you a hookup with a girl who is fertile and never wants to see you again, if you're lucky. But if you want any sort of ongoing affair, you need to also bring status to the table.

One way to have status is to...well...have status. If you're a Fortune 500 CEO and can string two words together, you'll probably do okay. But if you're a midrange worker, or blue collar, you need to establish status through speech, clothing, and behavior.

Some groups have their own standards. A power suit won't get you far at a line dance place, but $800 snakeskin boots, a solid silver tie clip, and a perfectly maintained Stetson might.

Do what you need to to distinguish that you can afford her, to send the subtle subconscious message that coupling with you is not engaging in the strong risk she will spend the winter pregnant, alone, and in the snow.

Money isn't the only marker of power or value

Some real-life roles convey power, like Judge, or Policeman. Some roles such as EMT convey the ability to face danger bravely which is a sort of power and value. Very fit men convey value because they seem strong and capable.

Men with an excellent skillset seem valuable because it seems like they would never want for work which means never want for food. An artist may seem valuable for the same reason, if he is admired or has a following.

Social leaders are often admired, though if you are having affairs in your own social group that can present a strong risk.

Think about the things that make you valuable and consider ways to point the up without overt bragging.

Decide who you are

At some point you are going to have a decision to make. Who are you?

Literally?

There are two ways to go about cheating, or arguably three, and the core decision is heavily based on what you want to get out of it. The core question is whether or not to adopt an alternate identity when you go cheating.

Investigation Discovery as a television enterprise has managed to make the idea of any adult American adopting an alternate identity tantamount to tattooing a swastika on your forehead and taking "Helter Skelter" as your life creed, but the fact is that plenty of people use alternative identities for a variety of reasons.

Your Options

Be yourself

For some things this is a no brainer. If you're going to hit the one airport bar in your small town, or plan to cheat with your sister-in-law, or grad student, you can't represent yourself as someone else.

Beyond that you have options. If you're planning to cheat in a big city, another city, or while traveling, you may benefit from being a "non person" who can't be easily followed or checked up on. This is a very strong positive if you plan to conduct one night stands or short affairs, and can still have some uses even if you plan on a longer term affiliation.

Note that you're going to need to do some of the work for creating a new identity even if you have no intention of posing as someone other than yourself, so don't let the work dissuade you. It's about the best strategic choice.

Be "someone else" soft option

If you're lucky enough that this can work for you, it can be the all around easiest option, however it works on the hope that your birthname has some viable variations. For example, let's say you were born John Fitzgerald Kennedy.

If you already go by Jack Kennedy to everyone at home, simply changing to using John Kennedy or J. Fitz Kennedy when you're away may work well. This works best if you have a fairly common last name.

For purposes of hitting the meet market in your city you become Jack Fitzgerald. It's not that someone who ran into you wouldn't recognize you. It's the fact that they aren't looking for you. If someone writes a teary tweet to her friends about having been ditched by Jack Fitzgerald, it isn't so likely to end up at your doorstep.

There are myriad advantages here. If your partner ever looks at your Driver's License, it will probably "check out" as correct.

It's easier to use your real last name. Some banks are flexible enough that they allow you to enter which names show up on your Credit Card. You may be able to get a card that says "Jack Fitzgerald" or at least "John Fitzgerald," fairly easily.

If your name is Neiphiu Brahmpura it's a little more difficult. You may be able to take advantage of the fact that many

Americans don't understand non-European names to convince a bank to print your name backwards on your credit card "that is my family name," or to convince them that a completely different shortened form is "the same." If you've been "Neff" you could become "Brahm."

Almost every name has permutations. At worst you could turn Drew Millhouse Zdinkski into "D.M.," and as long as you stay away from gamer geeks you should be fine.

Minimize contact with your ID

Try to avoid letting your affair partner see your ID. This can be very difficult if you sleep with them in the same place for several days, as hauling your wallet into the shower looks suspicious. Probably the best practice is to get a good quality locking briefcase and lock it in there when you are not out and around. That also allows you to stow any laptops, tablets or other devices which might not be sanitized, as well as the inevitable paper, bills, etc.

So that you don't seem too paranoid, you can set some ground rules. When staying at hotels (or other rented properties) mention that cleaning staff often work as "carders" scanning the cards of guests and selling them to an exploiter who will max them out over a couple of days. This is a real thing, and is actually a good reason to keep your cards locked up in a hotel. Why do it when you first come in? Otherwise you might forget, go to the pool, or get distracted. It may help if you have an expensive appearing watch (you can get an imitation Rolex for about $175 on the internet) or other valuables that seem to warrant locking up.

If that's too extreme, simply leave your wallet in your pocket, or tuck it deep into an inner recess of your suitcase. The sort of place that it would take some time and digging to find.

The most difficult situation is going to be checking into a hotel on trips. She'll want to stand there at the desk with you, and often the clerk will leave your ID flopped down in plain site as they read it. Working out ways to split up during check in, sending her to buy something from the snack kiosk, planning ahead and checking in before meeting her, etc. are all possibilities. The clerk is also going to call you by your name, and you'll have to correct them.

Have an excuse

Plan for the fact that your "real" name may come out, particularly if you're concealing your last name. "My mother's family were the Fitzgeralds, my dad was a Kennedy. But he deserted my mom, and I only use his name on my driver's license and bank checks. I've looked into changing it, but it would be too hard at this point."

Or "my Cousin was John and was always trying to top me on things. I didn't want to be the second John, so I use J. Fitz."

If you don't make a huge deal of it, likely she won't either.

Often it can be easier to share your "real" name as a secret early on, so that it's merely a curiosity when it comes up at hotels or other places that both check ID and use your name.

Summary

The idea here is not to throw off law enforcement, the idea is simply to create a filter so that any conversation, social media mentions, etc. about you are not likely to trace back to your actual account. You might go so far as creating an alternative Facebook page for yourself.

A slight change of name or emphasis in your name is probably your best bet for covering your tracks without undue complication.

Connections are weird. We knew a man who dated a girl in Chicago who did not choose to reveal her full name. It turned out, however, that they had a friend who had a mutual friend on Facebook.

Be "someone else" hard option

Here we get into secret agent territory.

You actually get ID that says you are someone entirely different.

First of all, let's be clear. In many states, possessing a fake ID is against the law. In most it's a misdemeanor, but in a few it's a class 3 felony. So...think seriously. We do not ever recommend that you present any fake ID to the police for any reason. Better to get a divorce than go to jail, and the odds are you can clean up a mess if you can stay out of lockup.

The good news is that you probably won't go to jail in either case.

You can get a fake ID off the internet for about $45-200. If you don't know how to do that, start by looking for "Deep Web" on Reddit, install a VPN and Tor browser and go from there. It won't fool cops (since it won't be in the state's database) but it will work on most everyone else. The good models have holograms and scan. But you can keep a fake ID at the top of your wallet and let your partner "see" it once or twice, after which there will be no real interest.

For more money you can actually get the core documents to establish a new identity, and get a driver's license issued in that name.

Test your Fake ID early. Go into a liquor store with a box scanner, and make sure it comes up as valid. If it comes up as invalid, try to get it back, say you've had problems with it before, and leave gracefully.

Presuming it scans okay, you can use your fake ID to check into hotels, enter clubs, buy alcohol, etc.

Just one problem. The credit card.

Opening a bank account with a fake ID is essentially a terrible idea. You are certain to get caught. Banks check everything, just like the police.

The best solution is probably to carry a prepaid card. If you prepay for hotel through Orbitz or other services, and only hand the card over for incidentals, it should have enough balance to keep you from having trouble. Carry enough for a room deposit in cash if you aren't certain. Prepaid cards will work everywhere else, and you can easily come up with a dozen reasons you use a prepaid card.

We recommend that you carry your real DL in the back of your wallet and your "girlfriend" DL somewhere in the middle. If you're stopped by a real cop, present your real license. The odds are that the girl won't notice, if you hand it directly to the officer.

The hard option works poorly if you use your own vehicle or have an affair near your house. It is better for ensuring vacation flings and high testosterone hookups remain comfortably distant.

All in all we only recommend this option if you already need it for other reasons. If you do, please read online, buy books and soak up all the information about the subject before putting yourself at risk.

Other options

Mysterious stranger

Being a mysterious stranger has its virtues. Simply refusing to show your ID can make you aloof and alluring. Some guys combine this with claims to be involved with intelligence, crime, etc. We really don't recommend this. It turns "who you are" into a hotbutton issue and unless it's a one night stand (in which case, she doesn't care who you are), you will eventually be found out. It undermines your apparent strength by making you appear to be afraid of "discovery" without any real benefits.

Kink community

One interesting thing which could be helpful to you is the existence of an organized "community" around Kink and Fetish, mostly coordinated through Fetlife.com. This can be useful if you have a few kinks, but be aware that women there are often disappointed with "vanilla" men who just want to have sex.

The positives? Keeping your identity secret is a core community value. No one expecting to play in public space (which may include sex in some places) is going to expect to learn your real name. Clubs are held to high standards of not disclosing the names of members who show ID at the door. You can give only a first name, a fake first name, or a "scene name." We recommend using a name that sounds plausible like "Scott" rather than something idiotic like "Whipmaster," but your mileage may vary.

The point is that "outing" people in "real life" is considered a major violation, and you could go very far down the path of dating without being asked about your real identity by a partner.

Complications

The wedding ring

If you opt not to be yourself, there's a major issue. Unless you aren't in the habit of wearing one, if you are cheating on a wife, instead of a long term partner, you have a ring on your finger. And it doesn't go away when you take it off. It leaves a mark as clear as day even after several months

You're going to have to explain it, because she's going to see it. One option is to cover it up with a class ring (Ebay) but that's so obvious most women will guess, and class rings are typically worn on the right hand because wedding rings go on the left.

Get your story ready. Many men are divorced, even long divorced, but your finger is going to suggest a recent parting of ways and there is no remedy for that.

Know your environments

If you're already having an affair, you could skip this section. Or you could read it as it might give you ideas about better possibilities or the dangers in your current situation.

Our typical picture of an affair has to do with meeting a glamorous looking girl in a hotel, or on a train, or in an airport, far from home. That may have been the case in the 1960s, but more than a half century later, that's no longer the case.

In the past we met potential partners of any kind through co-workers, high school and college, family, neighbors, or church. Now, according to Sociologist Michael Rosenfeld, we don't anymore. We meet partners through friends, at a bar/restaurant, or online. Moreover the share of friends is falling and the share of bars and online is rising sharply. The data is already about seven years old, so the change is likely becoming even more pronounced by the time you read this.

You're going to meet partners for affairs in very much the same way. That's dangerous because "through friends" is a difficult proposition for affairs. It means that the other person in your life knows your wife, and is in a position to easily disrupt your social constellation if they don't get their way. It may mean that a falling out would drag down your other friendships, split your life.

Below we'll look at the pros and cons of some of the places to look for affairs.

Target environments

Close to home

If you've ever heard the phrase "don't shit where you eat," it was meant to apply here. The worst possible place to go looking for affairs is right under your spouse's nose. Close relations (your sister-in-law), long time family friends, your daughter's friends from college...All very bad choices.

The reasons are obvious. There is a lot of opportunity for discovery, and the consequences are terrible. The explosion happens not only between you and your spouse but in the middle of your world.

That said, a lot of classic affairs are of this sort. We get interested in the people we're in proximity to. Our brother's wife. Our wife's sister. The family friend.

Most of the advice in this book still applies, as far as it goes, but really your affair is just a matter of time and place. You need to be in the same place at the same time, for long enough to have sex. Often that's incredibly easy to arrange. But read our sections on dress and redress and warnings on souvenirs and jealousy particularly well.

Avoid "exciting and dangerous" risks like having sex while your spouse is just down the hall and other exploits. Try to establish that secrecy and safety come first.

Aside from that there is little to say about this kind of affair. It happens not because you went out and worked to meet someone but because passion brought you together.

The nearby world

Work, hobby interests groups, the softball team, adult ed classes, all the other places that lay very close to home. For the most part these can be treated the same as any other place, with two exceptions.

First if you aren't already involved with someone, be careful about hunting so close to your own backyard. If you have to make several passes at people in a fairly small pond, you can get a reputation, and that might get communicated back to your spouse, or cause friction within the group. If these groups aren't singles driven, jealous monogamous men or women may call attention to you, or even set you up to fail. If they are singles driven, you may be one of several men circling as sharks, and have to fight for what you want or get involved in pointless fights that make your life more difficult.

Meet markets

So, this means bars/restaurants. Here's the bad news. Most of the games and activities are designed for singles. There aren't a lot of "married trolling for married" or "married trolling for single" nights.

The problem? Women meeting you are going to assume, based on your presence, you are available. "I'm still married" may be seen as a dealbreaker or even, after a couple of drinks be met with violence as a basic betrayal.

Some meet markets cater to an older crowd, and provided you are far from home, in a big town, or using an alternate name, you can probably risk passing yourself off as "in the process of getting divorced" if you are looking for quick action. The problem? If you come back to the same location, she will too.

"Trial separation" is a good status that gives you a chance to change things later. Instead of "I lied and said I was separated," it becomes "I have to give one more chance at this...I understand if you want to stop seeing me." If she's hooked and you didn't violate basic trust, she may be likely to agree.

Airport restaurants or places near convention centers my increase the chance of meeting travellers who are also married, or who expect you to be.

Unless you chose to go with having fake ID, you are going to risk giving your real name every time you pay the check.

Finding a good meet market can be tough. If you were familiar with meet markets before you married, you should have a fair idea of what to do. Just be more prosperous, better looking and more in control. If you never had much luck with such places juggling the extra issues of being married isn't going to make it easier.

Online

If you're not a super charmer who has the ability to approach dozens of women in order to size up the potential for an affair, the good news is that there are a lot of online sites that might be helpful to you. We're going to divide them into sites which specifically cater to people looking for affairs, and sites that are more general meet-market driven.

Affair oriented sites

The biggest issue with affair oriented sites is separating the wheat from the chaff. So, good news bad news. Women may be as inclined to have affairs as men, but they feel a lot less social permission to do so. I mean, guys who have affairs in movies are often cool, and even if they "repent" later they come out looking like the good guy. "Good girls" in films seldom cheat at all, and if they do they bitterly regret it. There is no female James Bond who casually sleeps with every man she meets, yet maintains self-respect.

That means that women are still more likely to hope they "fall into" an affair and less likely to put themselves out there. Still the situation is changing every year. Women feel more empowered to get what they want, and that means that there are real live women on dating sites.

Chatbots

Ashley Madison maintained a network of fairly complex chatbots that would occasionally engage customers with odd results. Some said the conversations had a sort of "soft porn" quality. You probably won't easily mistake a chatbot for a real woman unless you're very desperate, but, realizing after a while that those casual flirtations aren't real can be unnerving, and at first it is often hard to tell. We suggest asking a creative or off the wall question right away.

Fake profiles

Most sites, especially the smaller ones put hundreds if not thousands of fake profiles up to inflate their numbers. Often these are brilliantly easy to spot, as they feature porn actresses and rather simplistic profiles. Some go to the trouble of stealing pictures of average looking young women, but the fakes are still fairly easy to spot. They're generally unmanned and don't respond.

Professionals

Many of the profiles will be cam girls who want you to do a cam show with them. You're not getting laid right now, so why not take a little time and whack off over the internet? That's your choice, but generally cam shows are expensive.

A few will be professionals who are offering services, discreetly. There's no downside to that, but if you wanted a professional you'd be better off looking on TER where they are reviewed. It's amazing how many men will consider a "classy" prostitute who talks about wanting a "sugar daddy" on a "respectable" site, who are appalled at the idea of a two hour booking through an escort site. If anything girls who advertise on TER are less likely to be "scamsters" of some sort.

Site legitimacy

In general, the sites that you are more likely to find women on are the ones you can imagine a woman would use. If a site promises "Real MILFS, ready for action!" in the sidebar of your porn site, do you seriously think that a lot of women will go there? Do you know a lot of women who go around talking about their MILFhood?

There is no great pool of fantasy hotwives and cougars and desperate MILFs out there just waiting to let you dip your wick because you are available and capable of ejaculating sperm. It's not a thing. Many middle class men have this idea that there is a sea of lower middle class women, who are in poor earning and income situations who are desperate for a little bit of their action.

If you're prepared to actually be a full scale sugar daddy, maybe. Otherwise, those girls are not going to be impressed because you take them out to a nice dinner. This isn't 19th century London and they aren't Eliza Doolittle to be awed by the fact you have nice clothes. The last thing they need is one more freeloading guy in their lives.

In evaluating a site, we suggest three criteria:

1) Does it look like an actual woman would go there? Women understand that the type of men they meet on largely porn driven sites is not going to be worth the trouble. Does it feature pictures that show couples involved in an affair, or pictures that you'd expect to find on a porn site? Even if a woman is okay with porn, nothing about those images says "you are going to find decent men here."
2) Does it have references at the bottom to magazine and news articles, and are the legitimate? Sites that actually get traffic also get reviewed in online publications and even if the

reviews are negative, they usually trumpet that coverage. When you google the site, do other hits or articles in real publications like The Guardian, or Huffington Post come up, or is the only coverage of it obscure "adult dating" blogs?
3) Does it feature information about women on the front? You are looking for phrases like "Women owned" or other language that suggest it is a site targeting actual women, rather than a site trying to lure horny guys with *pictures* of women.

All sites probably have a few legit profiles, but low end sites don't have many, and some may have none at all. Do your homework by googling references to the sites that have some public traction.

For low end sites, don't assume that your Credit Card information is safe, though it usually is. Use your "cheating card," which should have limited amounts of cash attached to it.

Legit opportunities

Some small proportion of the girls you encounter will actually be women interested in having an affair. At this point you need to impress them, and the rules are pretty much the same as for any other dating site, other than not needing to deal with how to explain that you are married.

We'll talk about putting a profile together below.

The Ashley Madison hack and security

For some years there was really only one big contender, Ashley Madison. However the site was hacked in July 2015, and the real names of users, attached to their credit card information, was made public. The two results were that nearly every cheating man on the planet who knew about the internet had an aneurysm, and a lot of men stopped being willing to use dating sites.

Marriages were destroyed, especially those who attracted attention in conservative areas (one Alabama newspaper printed the names of all local residents on the site) or were identifiable political or religious figures. The fact is that the data was fairly hard to get through and most women never sifted it. Most people whose information was leaked remained unknown simply because no one knew or cared if they had actually had an affair, and there was no systematic way for the hackers to get that information to their partners.

While sites have beefed up security most are still vulnerable. The good news? There's no real obvious "big fish" like Ashley Madison and a few simple precautions will keep you safe:

a) Remember most people in the world have several others who share their name.
b) Give the nearest big city as your address.
c) Don't give your real birthdate.
d) Use your "safe card" to pay for any online charges. More about that in a moment.

Provided your wife doesn't already think you're cheating, even if there is another big hack on cheating sites, you probably won't be outed in a meaningful way unless you're a very high profile individual. If you are you might consider using a very heavily treated picture. And remember if your wife hits the same site, she might find you and it won't necessarily resolve in a mutual laugh.

Dating Sites

There are a world of mainstream dating sites of the "swipe left" variety. OKCupid is probably the best known, but there are literally hundreds of others. The problem is that you're competing with guys who are available.

Your advantage. Many of them have profiles that amount to, "I have nothing to offer a woman but my sperm and I will discharge that into any woman who is willing to speak to me."

You can outclass most people on a dating site. You need a top notch profile.

Constructing a Profile

There are hundreds of articles out there on putting together a good profile. Read at least four of them.

Key ideas

- Sell your strong points without dragging.
- Come off as intelligent and witty without trying too hard.
- Put as much information as possible.
- Use the best pictures you dare. Men without good pictures get responses. You're taking a risk if your wife also uses OKCupid "just to make fun of it with friends," or your single friend sees you.
- When you contact women, have an actual message that shows you read their profile, isn't trite, and isn't

condescending. Needless to say it should be in real English with words spelled out.

Don't do stupid things

- Don't have typos. Compose in Google Docs or something else that spellchecks, then cut and paste.
- Don't describe yourself as liking "books and movies." Everyone on the planet says that.
- Don't use a lot of profanity.
- Don't be sarcastic and world weary. Everyone does this. It makes you look like a pseudo-intellectual.
- Don't use language that's insulting to women. Yes, some women find that hot, but even the ones who like it in bed aren't so keen on it in a first greeting.
- Don't have a dead fish in your picture. Just don't.
- Don't wear a ballcap unless every woman you ever plan to date hangs with guys who wear ballcaps and likes it.

Dating Services

These sites go out of date almost as quickly as they come up, but here are a few that may have some actual profiles just to get you started

- Ashley Madison Revamped - ashleymadison.com
- Marital Affair - maritalaffair.com
- Married Secrets - http://www.marriedsecrets.com/
- Victoria Milan - https://www.victoriamilan.com/
- Hush Affairs - http://hushaffair.com/
- Illicit Encounters (UK) - illicitencounters.com
- Find New Passion - findnewpassions.com
- Gleeden - en.gleeden.com - claims to be woman owned

Special Interests

We mentioned kink site Fetlife.com above. It's really the only meaningful kink dating site, though a few others exist. Fetlife is legit and has recently cut some of it's more traditional kink content in order to pursue a more general audience.

Be aware of a few things:
- Most women on Fetlife get hundreds of requests for dates from vanilla men, and ignore them.
- The "looking in my area" groups are the best places to find potential partners. Post in the forums and comment intelligently and let women contact you.
- Kink is a community. Most of the women who spend much time there don't see it as a "meet market," and if you act like it is, they'll ignore you.

Sexting

As the internet moves along, photo sites like Kik and Instagram are becoming more popular with younger kids. Instagram provides some ability to send a photo that self-destructs after a set period of time...just remember anyone can take a photo of it, or use an app that captures the screen. These aren't hotbeds of cheating, but they're heavily used by singles, and you may find some venues for hooking up. They are used more heavily by cheaters to communicate, and we'll cover that under the technology section.

How your affair will look

Let's begin to talk about the core "feel" of your affair. What will it be like? This is where knowing yourself really matters because one affair doesn't look much like another Here we suggest some patterns of affairs, for you to begin thinking through how your affair will work.

You don't need to know exactly how your affair is going to be, but you do need to know which modes are unacceptable to you. And you and your partner need to have some agreement on where the affair is going. If it's a Junior fling to you but serial monogamy to her, you're setting up for a showdown.

Patterns of typical affairs

Comfortable friends with benefits

You are buddies who occasionally fall into bed. This works well, but is often easier for a man than a woman. Remember the core reasons why we're driven to sex. Providing some nurturing and companionship may offset the edge. Being the person she can vent to, or call for help in an emergency, particularly if it's acceptable to your spouses that you are platonic friends.

Issues: many movies have started with one partner in such an arrangement deciding that they need something more and that it's time for the other partner to get serious or give up. This can happen if either partner experiences a life event that causes them to want to fall back on the relationship. It's more likely if one partner isn't married and can lead to allegations of "wasting my life." It can also get old, and the burden of something more than a friendship can remain a matter of duty and obligation long after the sex has actually stopped.

Mysterious traveller

It's good work if you can get it. There's only one problem with this. If you aren't already good at seducing women, it's a bust. Essentially this is the solution if your issue is simply that you can have any women you want, and need not to shit where you live. Stella may be able to get her groove back quite easily with a man many years her junior, but if you haven't had success in the past, travelling with a wedding ring on your finger, or recently off it, isn't going to help.

Hookup apps may help you a little with this, but many a single man has taken an exciting and sexy vacation to find himself watching movies in an empty hotel room. Don't believe that dressing nicely and being somewhere you have no friends, and no real claim to importance, is going to suddenly make you sexier or more outgoing.

Playing with fire/close to home

A dangerous affair with someone inappropriate at work, near the home, etc. The issue with these affairs is always the endgame. They usually burn out, sometimes for one partner before the other, when the fear starts to overrun the thrill. That can leave a bad situation of effective blackmail, where one partner is pushed to continue the sexual relationship because the cost of anger or discovery would be too great. It can put longstanding friendship and stability at risk and make a pleasant household unpleasant. The best case is that both parties decide to "cool it off" at about the same time without ever having been caught.

Junior fling

You have an affair with someone who is very much your junior. Often a former student, a junior employee at work, or some other young person with whom you are in a mentor position. Probably the gravest issue with this sort of affair is that it is often much more serious to the younger person, though sometimes the reverse is true. The older man is a "fling" to be left for a more appropriate boyfriend. From the point of view of the older man, you need to do as much as possible not to set false expectations or "lead on."

An added complication to this is that in our current society we have begun to make hard and fast rules against this sort of thing. In the *Mad Men* days of Don Draper, it was expected that a boss might have an affair with a secretary. Now it may break social rules or professional association laws *even if both parties are fully aware and consenting.*

Playing house

You're really just playing at creating the idyllic life you hoped to have in your marriage. It's easy because you don't have all the things that come with marriage. Kids, budgets, pets, a dirty kitchen and laundry. A date night with your spouse might be worth considering. That said, there's nothing really bad about playing house but it can lead to very intense expectations. "Let's pretend" can easily be understood as "this is how our future together is going to be" and create the expectation of serial monogamy.

Serial monogamy

Whether you get divorced or not, you are looking seriously to jump ship. You are lining up the next Mrs. Right, even if you don't know it yet. Here your biggest danger is the break. You undergo the emotional shock of breaking with your wife and things change very badly for the new Mrs. Right. Formerly she was the candy treat, the exotic fun thing. Now you're crying on her shoulder and she's suddenly doing your laundry. You're no fun and she's got all the problems of the previous Mrs. Right so...you start looking elsewhere. Lather, rinse, repeat. If you don't change the basic behaviors, it isn't going to be different the next time, and if you can't be honest with yourself, you're setting yourself up for a long and expensive set of legal issues.

MAD

This is really an element that can be present in all the above scenarios, but we wanted to frame it out for you. In the Cold War, "mutually assured destruction" was the idea that since both sides had enough nuclear weapons to wipe the other off the face of the earth, and each side could launch their missiles before the enemy missiles arrived, a war meant that both sides would automatically lose. MAD is a situation where two spouses are having an affair, usually high tension, and neither can afford to spill the beans.

The downside? One spouse can decide to leave their marriage and suddenly there is no balance in the relationship.

Cheating based on mutual respect and a good healthy regard for the other partner's lifestyle is usually better than MAD.

This means that if you're not in the habit of showing your partners respect, you're not going to get much in return if she decides to jump ship and "corner" you.

The Technical Details

We've talked about affairs on a high level. Now we're going to get down to the grit. The things you need to do and know to conduct a successful affair

Method acting

In the Victorian era, melodramatic overacting was the rule in most drama. Between the turn of the century and 1930 Konstantin Stanislavski developed the prototype of acting and theater as we know it today at the Maly Theater in Moscow.

Most people who hear about it think it is about "living in character" even offset. That's never been true, though Stanislavski did experiment with the idea, so that's just not what we're talking about.

Yevgeny Vakhtangov created an important distinction, separating Stanislavski's process of "justifying" behaviour with the inner motive forces that prompt that behaviour in the character and "motivating" behaviour with imagined or recalled experiences relating to the actor and substituted for those relating to the character. Following this distinction, actors ask themselves "What would motivate me, the actor, to behave in the way the character does?

You need to become a method actor. You may be joyful about your upcoming date, but you need to be a man who is on his way to work. You also need not to attract attention by melodramatically overacting "oh God I hate these night classes!"

You need to capture your emotion at times that it is appropriate and learn to replay it when you are thinking about your dates.

One way to do this, and probably the best way is to think through your imaginary day before and after each date. Where did you go, what did you do, what did you see?

I left the house and drove to the airport. There I walked to the United counter, got my boarding pass, cleared TSA before the line got long (what was the TSA line like at that time of day?), and had a drink at the airport bar. I boarded United Flight 4707 (because you've already checked) and flew to Albuquerque, where there was a brief delay before flying to LAX. I got an uber from the lower level at LAX and went to the Quality Inn. (What did the rooms look like? You'll find pictures online.) It was still early when I got in, because of the time difference. The weather in LA was in the fifties, which was cold for them (you checked the weather online). I ate at the Panda Express.

You may have been at a Sheraton ten miles north of your house, but you know where you were and when you were. You have a mental image, a narrative you can fall back on. When you think of that narrative, think of the appropriate emotions. It may be stitched together of Googled information, memory of old business trips and imagination, but you need to infuse it with the right quality of slight apprehension, dullness. Think of a couple of stories, even if they are pointless. The clerk at Panda Express was very friendly. Your Uber driver was an immigrant from Georgia who talked a lot about hating Putin. Half-told stories and random off the cuff comments are the stuff of reality. Elaborate tales are not, unless it's your usual style.

You can decide for yourself about integrating elements of your real trip into your faux memories. Sometimes this can work well (it was LA, except the purpose was a girl and not a business meeting...or along with a business meeting). Other times it can lead to trouble. "You said it was raining...I thought it was sunny there all the time." In general the less manufacturing of stories you have to do the better, but don't go with the idea that "vague is good."

Constant vague answers ("where did you stay?" "a hotel") are maddening and suggest deception. Volunteering details "how was your trip," "okay, though the beds at the Miramar Suites are crap, I'm going to do the Sheraton next time," is a good way to establish credit before you're asked.

Intelligence people call this sort of comprehensive back story your "legend." Your legend is more limited, but that's a good way to think of it. Always have your legend straight, and practice thinking of and answering questions about it. Review it before you leave on your affair and before you walk into the house.

The excuse

On a one time basis you can make up a crisis or just bolt from the house, but if you are going to conduct any sort of long running affair, you need an excuse.

The excuse is also one of the hardest areas. You can tell yourself that it "doesn't matter" that you are cheating, but the excuse brings you face to face with the quantity and quality of time you are taking away from your spouse. Because of this, men often try not to think too hard about the excuse, which leads them to make mistakes.

You have already decided to lie to your spouse. Let's be clear about that. If you *aren't* okay with that fact, see above: reconciliation, divorce, polyamory. Even if you aren't saying "I'm not having an affair," if you're thinking of it as cheating, you're engaging in basic, core, dishonesty.

So own up and plan. If your reason for an affair is to get your needs met without hurting your spouse, the best way to do that is to make sure your affair is not a leaky disastrous mess that leaves her paranoid and guessing. You need to be spotless and clean.

One good idea is to come up with an excuse well beforehand, and put it into practice for a while before there is an affair date.

It is easiest if you break down your actual needs
- **Evenings** - free time in the evenings
- **Weekends** - free time on the weekends

- **Phone and Text** - reason to be lowly or non-responsive to phone and text, so that your spouse cannot disrupt your affair date constantly
- **Access** - guarantee that your spouse cannot show up at the place you are supposed to be
- **Information** - guarantee that your spouse cannot interrogate another person to reveal your lie, or that person cannot expose you by accident
- **Real World Support** - guarantee that no real world issues (mailing, phone calls from your boss, traffic tie ups, etc. will give you away)

Don't assume you are going to be able to conduct an affair in the afternoons with a woman you aren't paying. The woman who is sexy and available in the afternoon for businessmen is the legendary unicorn of the affair world. Nearly extinct, she's so rare that the last reported and confirmed sighting may be from 1973.

If you work as a professional and can take afternoons off, you may have the opportunity to date other professionals who can also take an afternoon off. Don't count on it. If your plan for cheating revolves around free afternoons, professional sex workers may be your best bet.

Phone and text

It's hard to overstate how much phone calls and texts from another partner can be a buzzkill on affair dates. The very occasional, very businesslike, call may be fine (ie. "sure I'll pick Sally up from school tomorrow afternoon"). But remember that every single call or text, ever furtive glance, is a reminder that she is sharing you with another woman, and that woman holds all the cards in your life. Whether you are the high testosterone predator, or the relationship man, you need to make her feel safe, and feeling another woman has your attention when you are with her does nothing of the sort.

It gets worse as the evening wears on. A younger woman may not care much if you check phone or texts over dinner. But having to check your phone as you fall into bed, or rushing to check it when you are done, is a huge buzzkill.

There are a few things you can do to help with this and get a bit of slack. Establish that you are on call at work, and attribute texts from your spouse to a less experienced developer, sysadmin, manager, or whatever works in your line of work. "I don't have to go in, I just need to call him for a few minutes and walk him through a server restart." Make sure your wife's texts do not light up with her name and number. There are a lot of text management apps, especially for Android phones, that don't show graphics, install one if your own phone's display is garish.

In the end, limiting communication from your spouse is imperative. It's helpful if your spouse isn't the sort to call or text very often, but if not you need to come up with reasons she cannot get through. Maybe you work in a server room that is a faraday cage and get poor reception there. Maybe you are in a meeting (at what hour!) and can't take calls.

The problem with alibis

One of the most common excuses is being "out with the boys" and that gives rise to a ton of issues. It's helpful if going out with the boys is in fact something you've done, but presuming you aren't going to suddenly ditch on them, you're still going to be upping your commitment.

While a friend your wife doesn't see too often is a good alibi, it needs to be a friend who won't call when you are with them, or accidentally blurt out details "I took Clara to see a movie last weekend?" "Oh really I thought you were fishing with Jake in the mountains."

There is no real good system with alibis. A friend who doesn't know they're your major alibi is prone to accidentally give you away. A friend who does know they are your major alibi might give you away through nerves, or worse, gossip to a trusted female friend. If you have the type of friend who has been seamlessly vouching for you since High School, who you know adheres to "the code" and would never talk out of school, you may be good. Otherwise, avoid friends as alibis if you can.

Working late

Probably the world's most common alibi is working late. It is the one benefit of living in a culture where men work more unpaid hours than any other developed nation. It often works for women as well as men. That said, there are some real issues.

Your work is typically a fixed place. Can your spouse come by to see if your car is there? Can your spouse actually walk in on you? Is it the sort of place where anyone else works late? What are you working on? What are you working on, late into the night, that requires you to be dead on text and phone?

Working late is one of those excuses that seems golden, but often leads to getting caught in the end. It's too comfortable and too easy and eventually you make a mistake. Ultimately your jobsite is a trap, and your phone availability at the jobsite is a major issue.

It helps if you have a job that would be hard to check. For example, if you happen to work at a secure facility with underground parking, it might take quite a stakeout or private detective to prove you weren't working there.

If you work in a datacenter with thick walls, claiming that your phone is dead when you're in the server room is a decent excuse.

It helps if your job moves around. If you do cable installations, then being unable to call from certain locations, and being nowhere in particular become much more understandable.

Of course, you're not limited to the actualities of your job. You're just limited to what you can reasonably say your job entails. So, for example, you could begin having to do offsite work at a contractor facility. That might even require occasional overnights. You could be asked to do a scheduled training every thursday night at a local college arge enough that finding you without the room number would be essentially impossible.

How well your wife knows your co-workers and is involved with your work life will dictate a lot of this. If she's very heavily meshed with your fellow employees, cheating at work is a very bad idea, or at least no safer than cheating with her best friend or an in-law.

Out of town trips

Out of town trips can take a lot of the pressure off relationships, as it gives you a large block of unencumbered free time. Of course, there are a number of things to consider. Many of the considerations depend on whether you are actually going out of town, or merely using that as an excuse to cut free of your house for a day or two.

"Going out of town" locally works better in big cities. It's much easier in Chicago than Cleveland, and easier in Cleveland than Boise. The bigger the town, the less chance you'll run into your spouse, a friend of hers, or relations of any sort.

Consider issues like where your in-laws live, and don't count on big crowds to provide complete anonymity. Even if you stay at home, try to stick to parts of the city you don't frequent. If your town has several big suburban hubs, hit the ones furthest from your own.

Issues of payments and hotel are always an issue, but we'll talk about the technical details and what you'll need to be able to pull off a life of cheating.

If you're traveling for business, but actually taking days off work, consider how that is going to impact family vacation.

You can't kill vacation days you are already obligated to spend with the kids in Orlando. If you're going into work during the days, is that going to cause a problem? Will your wife hear from a friend that "Bob was at work all week?"

Actually being out of town is a lot safer, but brings its own suite of problems. You're more likely to be vulnerable to issues that give away your actual location, especially if it is different than the one that "work" is supposed to have taken you to. Try whenever possible to give your actual destination. If not you've got a lot of sanitizing to do...more about that in a minute.

Raising the possibility of a last minute out of town work trip is always a good idea. Sometimes things happen in your cheating relationship. Your partner has a meltdown. You must help them in an emergency or lose face. Sometimes you just need to fall off the grid for a day or so. If you've already established that you keep a hanging bag packed "just in case" it won't be a big surprise and you won't have to spend extra energy coming up with excuses while you are dealing with other problems.

If you ever plan to use this excuse, then use it once or twice a year, even if you go to a Motel 6 and watch cable. Having it be a thing that *can* happen makes it less suspicious when it *does* happen.

If you travel to a location different from the one you are pretending to travel to, use the internet to keep abreast of weather, and if you are sending email, don't forget to fix any "incorrect" time zone issues.

Night classes

Night school, especially followed by study groups, can provide a nice excuse, particularly if the person you are cheating with steadily goes to bed fairly early, isn't looking for a long evening, and is okay with a very set weekly schedule. Coming in at 2am from your "night class" is going to set off alarm bells from the very beginning.

We'll talk in a minute about supplementary material, but consider the reasons you are going to school and the positive benefits it will get you. If you're expecting a promotion, and it doesn't come through, there may be pressure on you to drop the night classes. Night classes eventually end, or at least change, but the schtick should give you a couple of years to consider better options or see if the affair is going to last.

If you're going to school, it should either be for credit towards a far off degree that you'll always fall short of (and that in itself can be an issue in a long term marriage) or better for technical certifications that your spouse doesn't understand or know much about. If you decide on certifications, do your research and know enough to talk informally if the topic comes up at dinner.

That said you may want to invent a certification that sounds like an existing one, but is specific to your company, or trade. Having your friend at dinner blithely mention that he managed to get his MCSE in 2-3 months when you've been working on it for two years will cause you ridicule at best, and grave suspicion at worst. Read up on actual certification programs, and build one that might be workable for your trade.

"Management improvement" classes that run for a full semester, and end simply qualifying you for a certification such as PMP, or NPMA. You might pass off certs you already have but never mentioned, or simply say that the company rewards you if you stay in "improvement classes." CRISC, CISM, various Certified Solutions Architect certs, CISA, CCNP etc...the list goes on and on. If you work in a specific trade, it should have industry certifications and improvement classes.

Second job

A second job isn't unlike a Night Class, but it can allow you to stay out later. The downside? You're expected to bring in some extra money. There are a couple of options in this regard. One is to balance it with something the money is paying for which can't be established. If you own the house and your partner isn't on the mortgage, you could say that the escrow had gone up by $400 a month, but you were going to offset it by taking a night job.

If you work in IT, it may make your partner think less of you if you suddenly take a job as a night watchman. Be inventive if you can. "I've been offered a contract position two nights a month. There's a server farm out on the Golden Corridor. Their regular manager gets one night off a week and they need somebody experienced to babysit. It's not much money, but it's just six hours of boredom and doing the occasional reboot most of the time. Of course I can't take personal tech in with me. They have some government stuff there."

If you can pass off that you're working as a security guard do. Beware of easily checked jobs like restaurant work. What if your spouse took pity on you and decided to come by and bring you a midnight snack? Security, night management, even custodial work is probably better.

A second job is better than your primary job because you can even ask your wife to keep it a secret from any work pals. "It's not against the law, or even company policy, but if they found out they'd want to wring more hours out of me." She won't expect to know anyone at your new job, or for there to be much social life around it.

Integrated excuses

We know one cheater who took a second job to pay for his night school. The certifications from his school put him on course to a promotion, which he was already expecting but called for...more classes to get up to speed.

Sports and hunting

A lot of men who are already fairly independent rely on sports or hunting as an excuse. The theory is that "time with the guys" isn't threatening, and the wife may well want you away from the house now and then.

This can have a lot of downfalls. Sports revolve around events, which may be attended. Solo sports such as kayaking may still entail a lot of interest or the desire to see you. Make sure it's a sport you're actually competent at. Golf is a possibility if your spouse tolerates overnight golf trips

er along. Otherwise it may provide an
afternoon break which can work with the right affair.

These things tend to involve needing partners to support an
alibi, with drawbacks we've already discussed.

One big warning here is to make sure to take all the
appropriate equipment, or at least make noises if you forget
it. "Yeah, I had to use one of the cheap tour wetsuits since I
left mine in the bathroom." **Do not skimp.**

If you're going to be fishing for three days, take all the
necessary supplies and come back with them looking a little
the worse for wear, not exactly as you packed them. You
may think your wife isn't smart enough to know or figure out,
but things in our environment that are "wrong" may set off
unconscious alarm bells.

Supplementary material - mail, etc.

Having access to a laser printer, and Word, or Photoshop,
can be helpful if you are literate and understand business.
Buying some window envelopes and sending quarterly
reports, bills, or other random contact information from your
school can be very helpful. Running off an envelope with a
logo on it takes about ten minutes in Word, and it will add a
ton of credibility to your story.

Even if these things seem silly, real world confirmation of
your plans can be important.

Think of it this way. Let's say that your friend Bob seems a little mysterious. He is out of town at times, and you've noticed he keeps a gun in his glove compartment. He's a nice guy, no problems. But you're very suspicious. Finally a situation comes up at a bar one night where you see him hit another guy in an alley. When you approach him, he tells you that he works for the CIA, and that you shouldn't talk about what you saw.

Okay...maybe that's true. Or maybe he works for the mob. All your alarm bells are going off.

But what if you'd been to Bob's home? You'd seen that he was a decorated military officer from pictures on the wall of his study. You already knew he had firearms, and you'd actually seen his Federal ID when he was paying for dinner one evening. You've already concluded he is a spook of some sort, so it's less of a reach when he gives his alibi. Your mind is already working to fill in the gaps.

In fact for all we know Bob could be a con-man. But your mind is perfectly prepared to accept his story. In fact it's been building Bob's story for him.

Seeing mail, getting souvenirs from places you haven't been (ebay to your office) and other solid artifacts do a huge amount to establish certainty and make sure your alibis will never be questioned.

Collecting data

In the 1960s and 70s, Eastern Bloc intelligence officers in the US often travelled away from their embassies. Operating with diplomatic immunity as "cultural attaches" or "military liaisons" they had a rather strange ritual. Whenever they arrived at a hotel, they'd neatly bag up all the stationery, pens, matchbooks, and any other "free" items, label it, and take it back to the embassy where it was shipped to Moscow or kept on file by the Resident. Later, sometimes years later, they might need to make an alibi, or establish that someone had been in a place at a time for one of their "assets" who operated without diplomatic protection...the actual spies.

You might want to do the same thing. Visiting a place that might be an alibi? Take pictures. Grab flyers or other documentation. Visit the college where you take night classes and pick up some random literature, often found on boards in departmental halls. Buy a bag, or buy something at the gift shop. Keep a pile of "evidence" to drop casually to maintain your facade.

Pictures may be especially important, and a few casual snaps to send home may be very helpful if you're on an overnight trip. Even better, random posts to Facebook with your selfie from the airport bar. "Waiting on my late flight." We'll talk more about photos in the tech section, including understanding that some photographs can convey information on when and where you were...which can be both a good and bad thing.

One Web-savvy fellow built a website for a faux conference. He paid $15 for a domain like Boise-Managementconference.usa, and hosted it with a hosting service that builds websites for you. He copied text from another conference site to make it seem "Authentic" and pasted in photos of the Conference center from another event at the same place. For a final touch he paid someone on Fiverr $5 for a conference logo. He then downloaded some other conference registration confirmation, edited it in word and left copies on the kitchen table with his other papers. He left the website up on his non-secret laptop. Emails went to his own address which had an auto-response prompting to login to the secure members page with a code provided in the registration email.

You could do the same thing with a school curriculum or series of management classes, giving you weeks or months of "nights off."

Voicemail

Getting "work" to call you in occasionally might be a good idea. Or getting your school to call. On services like Upwork.com or Fiverr.com, you can find people who will make telephone calls for you. To get them to call your wife, provide them with a script and have them make a test call. The script should be realistic and non threatening. "Hi this is Nadim making a courtesy call from Local Community College. May I speak to John?. Oh, that's fine, please just remind him that registration for the spring semester is only one week away." Or even "could you ask him to call the registrar's office to update his payment record."

Sanitize

After your date your biggest job is to sanitize. Everything.

Your clothes. Your skin. Your mind.

You must wipe the thing that just happened out of existence. This can actually be emotionally painful for some men, and they tend to resist it. That's a problem. Here's a checklist for sanitization.

Is your skin clean?

A full shower is best, but if not, consider unscented baby wipes. If you can't shower, saturate your crotch area, and try not to take your shorts off near your wife until you've showered. In a pinch clorox wipes are hard on the skin, but they'll do and you won't die.

Is your hair dry

A shower is great but why is your hair wet? Make sure if your shower close to home that you use a blow dryer, or have a decent excuse for having just showered. A late stop at the gym is always workable if it fits into your overall life pattern.

Dress and redress

Clothing may be a big part of your affair. The issues:
● You need to dress dapper on dates, but leaving the house dressed for a date is suspicious.
● Things are passionate, but that means hair on your collar, her perfume on your sport coat or shirt, even fluids on your pants leg or crotch.

Scent is a much bigger factor than you may think. It may be "just perfume" to you, but women are often able to discern a lot of scents you can't or don't. Another woman's perfume may be a massive alarm bell. The smell of sweat or sex on you may be very noticeable.

Taking off your underwear with another woman's fluids on you, even if a condom was involved, may be the equivalent of taking a spray bottle and blasting your spouse's face with "I just cheated" gas.

Do not assume that because you can't smell it, she can't smell it, even if you have a better appreciation for the scent of your favorite red wine than she does. Some smells are "invisible" to men, because they exude them. Just like you get used to the ticking of a clock, you may be unable to notice your own musk.

The clothes that have been in contact with your partner's body are going to reek of her to another woman. Even if your wife doesn't consciously recognize the scent, the unconscious hint may be what sends her down the trail to suspecting infidelity. Add to that that your clothes may smell of places you should not have been, for example of liquor and smoke if you went to a bar rather than a classroom. You need to not be wearing them, and you certainly need not to leave them for your wife to launder. Even if you've gotten away with it before, it's a terrible practice.

You may overlook hair that your wife notices with ease. You may fail to notice scents. Change your clothes. At absolute worst, go immediately to change and shower and bury your cheating clothes at the bottom of a pile of sweaty laundry. Much better, change to fresh clothes before you hit the door.

Solutions

You need to plan ahead. The easiest thing may be a clothing change on your way to the date. Here are some suggestions:
- A 27/7 gym can be really useful. They provide a locker, you may even be able to store "date" clothes there, and you can shower before and after. Unfortunately not everyone has an all hours gym a convenient distance from home or office
- Some offices have gyms with changing rooms. If your excuses involve "working late" a check in before and after
- If you're on a budget or travelling, it's worth knowing that most large truck stops have clean showers. While they say you have to be a truck driver to use them, they don't care and don't ask. If they say anything, which is a one in one hundred chance, say you are doing a management inspection of some fleet assets and not driving a rig right now. The websites of the major chains (Pilot, Flying J, TravelCenters, Loves) will help you find locations, and if you live in a fair sized city there are probably stops just at the periphery of your major highways. The showers aren't fancy, but they're large, clean, and also offer places to shave.
- Dry cleaning is your friend. One good trick is to keep your "date suit" in a hanging bag folded neatly in the trunk of your car, or at your office. Your reason? Sometimes you get sweaty and are called into a late afternoon meeting, have to go on overnights for work with no notice, etc. Make sure the bag won't be opened (throw a TSA lock on it, with complaints about the custodial staff swiping a $30 tie), and rotate outfits to the dry cleaners without ever letting them enter your house.
- While most bar and restaurant bathrooms say "no changing" nobody ever actually stopped someone from changing. If you go into the largest stall with your hanging

bag, and come out differently dressed, no one will know or care. Tear off one of those toilet seat covers to stand on so you don't end up in sodden socks.

• If you stay at a hotel, consider trying to run a load of laundry the last night, and keep a change of clothes that hasn't touched your date for the ride home.

Febreeze

Febreeze can be your friend in eradicating odors from your clothing or car, when you don't have time for a major wash. The downside? It has an odor of its own which is fairly distinctive. Some people keep Febreeze in an older car that has an occasional musty odor anyway. If not, it may be hard to explain, but used in moderation and driven with the windows open for a few miles, it should be fine.

Febreeze has a better cousin, which is cheap vodka mixed with water. Theater departments use this to spray down costumes between a matinee and evening performance. The problem? It's open alcohol in a car, and if fresh may cause problems with a cop, especially if you actually have been drinking at all.

Temporary fixes

What you can't eradicate, conceal. In an emergency making a smelly mess may mask otherwise incriminating smells. Grabbing a beer and spilling it on your shirt when you first come in, having a late night PB&J to make sure you smell like peanut butter, may mask more offensive smells until you can get clean and get those smells into the wash.

Storage units

Many cities rent storage units with 24/7 access fairly cheaply. Often they're even climate controlled and somewhere there is a bathroom. You could conceivably make one of these your "gym" and a cheap hotel away. If you have sex at her place, but leave afterwards, too late to come home to your house, you could stay there, freshen up and come home. A couple of jugs of water and a basin served to bathe Victorian England, and you can keep a change of clothes there. You could also crash occasionally. The management isn't crazy about people living in the cubes, but if you just doss down occasionally you can put it down as an "all night work session" if you don't maintain a full bedroom. There's also no real consequence if you get thrown out.

Many of these units don't have power but most have lights so for running your phone, tablet, etc. you can go by a hardware store and get one of the old style bases that screws into a light socket and adds a power outlet. These won't handle hot plates or heavy machinery, but they're fine for computers or other things requiring minimal voltage, and will actually handle a surprising amount of current.

Objects

Make sure that objects connected with your affair are either in safe places or thrown away. This means condoms, lube, receipts, hotel bills, card keys, her leftovers, her cigarettes, etc. Everything and anything that is not a part of your day to day life. Large sums of cash taken out to spend. Anything.

If your date rode in your car, check the seat, thoroughly. Check under it and in the crack for lost earrings or any other misplaced bits of femininity. It is best if your date never rides in your car, but if they must, try to set up situations where some other women your wife doesn't know well might plausibly have ridden in your car. An out of town co-worker dropped at the airport. Anything that provides a reason why some artifact you overlooked has ended up on the floor of your car, or rolling around under the child seat.

Her scent will linger on the seat too, so don't forget about our lesson on Febreeze. If you have teenaged children and you have the option of taking a car they sometimes drive, do that.

Remember that objects are not just things associated with a woman, but things associated with the date. Why do you *have* a bottle of Febreeze in the car (obvious answer if it's an older car).

A locked briefcase or "spare clothes bag" is the place for any gifts, correspondence, sex supplies, or sex toys associated with her. Keep them in a ziploc bag so they don't scent your clean clothing.

Pocket items

A stunning number of men clean everything on their person, but leave evidence in their pockets. The card key from a hotel you weren't staying at. Receipts from a restaurant you didn't eat at. A condom. Check your pockets.

Supplies

What we said for hunting or fishing goes for any other undertaking. Pack the right stuff. Going to classes? Have a bag or briefcase and textbooks (buy older books on Ebay). Going on a business overnight? Take your work laptop and papers.

Make sure that your sports, vacation, or class supplies don't appear completely untouched. That's a thing that may not make a conscious impression but can contribute to setting off alarm bells.

Electronic Sanitation

Email

Your email is your identity today. You need a solid gmail address which is not linked to your primary account.

The host of Silk Road, Ross William Ulbricht "The Dread Pirate Roberts," did everything right. Except one time, very long ago, he used his personal email address in a post on a forum. Eventually his whole legend was unravelled back to that early post.

Get your cheating email and your cheating accounts and your cheating name, even if you don't have special ID. Use them. Do not cross the streams. Do not be emo and wreck them and then recreate them, though you can burn them down if an affair goes bad. Burning them down leads to mistakes when your lust reignites and all that work is undone.

Computers

We'll start with computers, the oldest of the devices we live and die by daily, and also the most complex. We'll start with this. *You need your own computer.* Period. Do not try to conduct, search for, or otherwise manage affairs on a PC you share with your wife or kids. Yes, it *can* be done. It's not a good idea and in the modern day, if you can afford an affair you can afford a personal laptop.

A cheap chromebook won't set you back much and will give you everything you need to handle your own affairs.

We won't go into OS security here. If you know how to run Linux, and handle computer security you don't need this section, and if you don't telling you that Linux is safer than Windows isn't going to help you at all. We'll assume you use a Windows machine or some kind of Apple device.

This isn't a complete guide to computer security, but a starting point. We suggest you read up on the topics below especially as tech changes every year.

Lock your PC

Using whatever system is native to it. On more modern versions of most PCs it isn't that easy to break into a locked PC, so if your wife isn't a network security admin, you'll probably be fine. If she is, you really probably need to stay away from using electronics to organize your infidelity.

Set a short timeout and don't leave the machine alone with your wife, even for a moment without locking it. You can say it's "force of habit" from work.

VPN

Install a VPN. This isn't strictly critical to your affair, but it's relatively cheap ($12.95 a month or less) and it means your local ISP (and any other machines on your network) cannot see what your machine is sending and receiving. This should mean that no matter what your wife or talented hacker daughter do on the local network, your traffic is safe, and it will also keep your boss from seeing anything you do on your office wifi, if you have that privilege. It may be overkill for an affair, but it's a bit of peace of mind.

Chrome

There are a lot of secure browsers these days. Chrome's incognito mode doesn't track what you do on the local machine, and that's probably good enough for you. The key is not to leave a footprint. Even if you always use your own laptop it may be impossible to keep other family members from seeing the screen and you don't want embarassing data to be saved, especially if you use the machine frequently.

Google voice numbers

Google may be out to take over the world, but they aren't out to expose your personal affair. Google Voice is a free service that allows you to have a phone number attached to your gmail. Any gmail. You should open a gmail account you use only for cheating, and attach a google voice number to it. If you change partners you can always create a new gmail account.

What's better? You can log into two Google accounts at once, so if you spend long periods of your time on your affair computer, away from your family, it's not a nuisance.

Your Google voice number can forward to any cellphone (or other number) and it takes about two minutes to change. Use your Google Voice number for your affair texts and calls, rather than relying on your burner phone.

Note that mail in Gmail is never truly deleted. It can always be searched out of trash, so don't start your affair in an email account your spouse may have access to.

If you love some other system, that's fine, but Google offers fairly solid reliability and a very shallow learning curve. It's hard to screw up.

VeraCrypt

This is an awesome piece of software that will encrypt your computer to a standard that intelligence agencies would find challenging. It has one kind of interesting feature which is the ability to hide an entire alternate operating system. If you're forced to unlock the computer you unlock the "safe" normal operating system (which you should use occasionally) rather than the interesting one which you use for your infidelities. It's overkill for an affair, but it could be useful if you have a suspicious spouse, and think she may demand to see your laptop, or if divorce is in the winds.

Keyloggers

There is software that can run on your computer, which can log your typing. That can reveal passwords, and correspondence. The trick? It has to be installed on a machine the person trying to log your keys has access to. The downside? If you log into a secret account on a machine you share with your wife, she could easily have installed the software to monitor you. That means your password could be recorded and she no longer needs access to your machine.

Phones

Let's explain the good news and bad news. The bad news is that real phone security is hard. The good news is that your wife is not the NSA. Her ability to snoop into your private records is limited at best.

Your phone tells people where you are. It may also be used as a microphone and several other things, as we've learned from leaked intelligence reports. But your wife can't make use of that, so don't worry about it.

Here's what you do need to worry about:
● Any sort of social apps that encourage "check ins."
● Waze and some other apps can share your location with other people in your "network" or tell them when you are driving.
● Find my phone apps can show not only where your phone is now, but where it has been.
● Google (more about this)

Really it is best not to use your phone when you are away on a date. The best security is to shut it off entirely. If you have to keep it on, in order to take emergency calls, try to check what apps are running and think through anything that would transmit your location.

Burner phones

Burner Phones are used by drug dealers because they can be purchased at a convenience store, activated by anyone, and are hard to trace. They may be a good solution to keeping your affairs separate.

Of course you have to explain why you have a second phone. Ideally you can say it is issued by work, even going so far as to print a small "property of" and "if found call" tag identifying your company (with the number being your Google Voice number - more about that in a minute).

Your "work phone" can be locked after a short period because it's set automatically...irritating, but nothing you can change.

If you actually have a work phone that may be a little more of a problem. Conducting an affair on your actual work phone isn't very smart, though in the long run, if you use some simple precautions, it may be safer than your personal cell.

Cameras

Cameras are one of the most interesting and truly dangerous pieces of technology in our world. If you are cheating, cameras are, basically, not your friend. This is especially true if you are in the habit of taking off the wedding band to deceive

A camera is proof positive or negative that you are in a certain place. If you say you're in class, but can't sent a snapshot that shows you there dressed as you are when you left the house, you're busted.

Of course because of that such requests are impolite. Draw lines on them early or you will never be free unless you can carry a Hollywood backdrop. On the other hand a snap from school (taken in the same clothes a week ago) and posted to FaceBook can really strengthen your basic background.

Cameras also have an ugly trick. They record a mysterious thing called EXIF data, which records what camera you're using, the time and the place using geolocation if it's available, which it usually is. Turning off GPS doesn't help since it can get pretty close just using wireless. Since this data is never seen or used by anyone or any apps, it seems to exist largely to help law enforcement. Even finding an app to read EXIF data can be tricky. For that reason most people aren't busted by it.

Not every upload preserves EXIF data, but many do.

These days there are apps that view and edit EXIF data. That may be helpful to you. You can simply strip the data, or even replace it with data you like better, such as making last week's picture from school this week's.
Don't ignore EXIF data, and don't post pictures anywhere without stripping it, or altering it, if it may betray you.

Google

Google rates its own entry, though you may want to consider emergent technologies like Amazon Alexa as they become more prevalent. Be aware that Google records everything you say near your phone. Even if it isn't supposed to be recording. That's not some weird conspiracy theory. It's just a fact. Don't believe us? Check for yourself. The good thing is that Google allows you to delete that history. If you know it exists.

For the Audio Page (which is hard to find from the main menu)

https://myactivity.google.com/myactivity?utm_source=help &restrict=vaa

If you don't see anything, great! That probably means you don't have the Google Search assistant working on your Android phone.

The easiest way to stop Google recording everything is to turn off the virtual assistant and never to use voice search. If you don't do this:

- At least turn it off on your burner/cheating phone
- Turn your main phone off whenever you are out cheating or
- Erase your Google History every time
- In emergency be aware of and use incognito mode

For all your activity:

https://myactivity.google.com/myactivity

You may also want to click the "Three Dots" to look at "Other Google Activity" which will include your location history. That produces a chilling map of every place you've ever been with your phone on. Also easy to delete. You can also pause location history at any point, producing a nice record proving you were never in Las Vegas.

Take a careful look at your privacy information here:

https://myaccount.google.com

For more information, here's an article from The Independent, June 2016: *http://ind.pn/2a65tmy*

Safe link, but if you're worried, Google: Independent, Google June 2016 Andrew Griffin

Other devices

The world is filling with devices that know a tremendous amount about us. Does your smartwatch know you have sex? Did it publish that intense bout of energy to a public web page? "So what's this honey, did you suddenly do a dance exercise in the middle of Business class?" Does it tweet your sex to the world. "Bob has done an intense bout of cardio - FitTracker 3.0." Does your car have a built in GPS that logs where you have been?

Think about these things, and plan on workarounds. Don't let old fashioned mechanical issues like Odometer readings undo you. "You said you were in business class all evening, but apparently you drove nearly 116 miles...did you take the long way to school?"

Most tablets and other devices which aren't explicitly manufactured by Apple are actually built on an Android device. For example, Amazon Fire tablets are actually just Android tablets. Their ability to run standard Android apps could be good..or bad. Keep devices locked, or turned off, unless you need them.

Occasionally fake a crisis

One way to make your situation believable is to occasionally fake a crisis. Try not to do anything too dramatic or too unpleasant, the idea is to establish a realistic background, not to make your wife miserable.

Having your car stall in the parking lot of the local community college one tuesday night. Asking your wife to meet you at the airport just before you fly out, and bring a spare suit. Make sure you have good excuse for not clearing security if she decides to stay and have a drink.

Check her alibi

If your partner is also cheating...or even just has nosy friends...that provides an uncontrolled angle by which you might do everything right and get caught anyway. Bill Clinton was brought down not by Monica Lewinsky, who remained quite loyal to him, but because Lewinsky bragged to her friend Linda Tripp.

The problem is that to try to run a spy school for a giddy girl who is interested in a whirlwind romance goes counter to the feelings of the things. If you crush sexual feeling underneath a ton of paranoia you may not have a very satisfying affair.

Read her well and try and have some balance. Say you want to help "keep her safe" by checking her stories and alibis, and suggesting improvements.

In general you have to trust her, but the more she trusts you and the more input you give, the safer you are. Just remember, any criticism or feedback needs to be given constructively. Lashing out by accusing her of "endangering you," will go nowhere and may in fact prompt her to do just that out of resentment.

Try to get her to use the best alibis possible, remember to erase evidence, etc. On car dates, you should take responsibility for counting condoms, wrappers, and the torn tops of wrappers. If you had sex three times, or used three condoms, you should have three used condoms, three torn packages, and the top of every torn package. If you don't there is evidence in your car.

Note that an affair is one time to litter. Trash cans are great, but do not take evidence anywhere near your house. If that means a bit of litter, try to make up for it by being a good citizen otherwise, but if you need to throw things under your car in a parking lot, do that.

Finances

ID

We talked about ID a ways back. You'll need fake ID if you intend to pass as another person, and that's illegal and dangerous in many places. Aside from that you may be able to play with getting ID issued in names that don't reflect the most common version of your name.

Accounts

You can't easily buy things (like this book) without arousing suspicion if you don't have your own Amazon and other accounts. Getting them shipped discreetly to your office is a plus.

Budget

You're going to need money for most affairs. Not trivial sums, but amounts that may impact the household budget. It's up to you to decide how problematic and fair this is. What you should realize is that even if she tolerates the idea of you have sexual intercourse, most women do not want to see their household budget...money that could go to them...going to your affair.

This means you need to conceal a good bit of money. This is really where problems start with most affairs. When it's just about kissing on the sly, that's one thing, but when you announce that the budget is tightening shit just got real.

You need to have a place that the money is going. If your budget can carry it that's all well and good, but if it's a stress and a strain, you need a good reason why the money is moving out of the budget, particularly if your wife is heavily involved in the finances.

If your wife doesn't really see the income, lying about a pay cut is one option. Another is hiding a recent raise. Others could include tuition, or a moderately expensive hobby if the budget bears that and she is allowed the same luxuries. An expensive new prescription might be a good cover, or picking up part of the expenses of a living relative (who won't be inclined to talk).

For a relatively inexpensive affair if you work downtown, parking could be an excuse. You claim an exorbitant parking rate at your building while actually parking further away at a much less expensive lot.

Some men have conducted affairs entirely by withdrawing cash at the grocery, drug store, etc., under cover of prescription purchases.

You can conduct your first few assignations on an emergency basis, but when it becomes a regular thing, you need to plan ahead.

Money

You also need a way to get the money in a form that you can spend it. One option that would work with the "pay cut" model is to begin direct depositing to a second account, one that only you have access to. One problem with that can be that statements are mailed to your house, however many banks now offer "email only" statements.

Don't count on that concealing an account however. The bank will still mail overdrafts and random junk mail to your address.

There are several ways to handle this. A good "private" card is an employee credit union card, and you can claim to have a small account that exists only for some work related purpose, for example saying that you got a better deal on an auto loan or insurance by opening a small account there. That makes the statements pro-forma. In an ideal world you could have them mailed to your office, but that's hard to manage anymore, though employee credit union notices might pass beneath the radar.

There are a few workable prepaid cards, but many are junk, aren't accepted everywhere, and come with high fees. Still, if you need to put down cash at Wal Mart they may work for you.

Here's what you need:
• A reason to explain why money is leaving the household budget, or conceal that fact
• A way to get your own money without suspicion. Direct deposit to a second account, periodic withdrawals disguised as something else, a planned expense that can be paid in cash, or where your wife won't see the transaction in your primary account.
• A way to store and spend your own money on your affair.

Make sure you carry enough money for all expenses. The last thing you want to do is create a sketchy ATM withdrawal someplace you definitely weren't on a shared bank account that your wife can see online or in print.

Dangers/Pitfalls

Your guilt

In MacBeth, Lady MacBeth cannot be freed from her guilt, and goes mad, washing her hands and crying "out out damn spot." In real life it is often not the women who are emotional wrecks but the men. Convinced that cheating is bad, men undo themselves through guilt by either confessing, or breaking off affairs in an ugly way that leads their partner to betray them.

Don't be stupid. We'll repeat: Women are less likely to forgive an affair than men.

What's more stupid is that it's often a cowards way out. The man doesn't even want to make his wife feel better, he wants the burden of guilt alleviated. He wants the long suffering angel who married him to wipe his brow and say "there there." He wants a mother.

In *Mulholland Falls*, Nick Nolte's tough guy cop explains why you don't tell a woman about an affair. "You carry your own water." What he means is that you chose the burden of guilt, you carry it. You're already cheating on this woman, taking away time and attention from her. Telling her about it just adds the *insult* of making her bear your guilt as *well*.

While most wives say they would "like to know," most people don't know what is good for them. What your wife would like is if you focused your attention back on her and your relationship and met her needs better. She might like the money you are spending on her affair. Or you may be meeting her needs and the problem may be, mostly, yours. In any case, you do not improve your life by being "honest" with her.

If you can't take your affair to the grave, don't have it. Cycles of cheating and confession always end badly and are never becoming. They are beneath your dignity.

Done cheating? Politely break with your partner in a way that makes you the bad guy and doesn't hurt her feelings. Don't make it about her, make it about you.

Then put that attention and money back into your wife. But otherwise do not burden her with your guilt, or make her your Priest to assign penance for your strayings.

Seriously think about the downside of cheating. Imagine not just the excitement of new flesh, but the feeling of sitting with your spouse knowing you have just been with another woman. How does that make you feel? If it is uncomfortable, think harder. Can you live with it? If not, do not follow this course of action.

Masochism - making it work badly

A stunning number of men set out to have an affair to make themselves feel better, but end up working it to make themselves miserable, either not enjoying the affair, or giving themselves away creating years of suspicion, paranoia, or divorce.

Why is this?

In Edgar Allen Poe's *Tell Tale Heart,* a man exposes his own act of murder because he imagines the beating of his dead victim's heart can be heard by everyone, a betrayal by his own morbid imagination and conscience.

Let's understand what conscience is. It's not an angel or devil sitting on your shoulder. If you've seen wild dogs eat, you'll see that some take more food than others, but no wild dog in a pack will take all the available food unless it is starving and there is only enough food for one. The reason is scientific and evolutionary. The dog pack is stronger with more members and can take more prey. If a few strong dogs eat all the food, they will starve the pack, or become its prey.

Yet you don't imagine a dog reasons about this, has an internal dialog. "Hmm...Yeller and Blue are quite useful in a scrap, and if we keep Blackie alive we could bring down larger prey. I'll stop eating now to ensure they stay strong."

Rather a biological driver kicks in a set of alarm chemicals including the stress hormone cortisol if the situation is one of taking "too much" and would create a danger.

This is our conscience, better developed and able to interpret our logical thoughts through our unconscious mind and gut.

Once one has embarked on a dangerous course of action, the unconscious mind may feel alarm. Indeed if one is alarmed enough by fear of discovery, fear of consequence, morbid fear of disease, the sense of alarm may become overpowering.

But why would *conscience* ever dictate that we undertake an action that is clearly grossly to our disadvantage. Give away an infidelity when the consequence is sure to be a great loss of status with our spouse or even divorce?

Three reasons

Release of tension

Our brain yearns to release tension that is causing us stress. In primal terms this is what causes a dog to roll on its back and bare its throat to another dog. It's a relief from stress that gives a reward. If we were dogs this would work well.

Anticipation of failure

We believe we can't succeed or might not succeed, so instead we submit ourselves to punishment.

It doesn't know better

Why would a man who only feared being caught surrender himself to the certainty of being hanged. The reason is that interplay between subconscious "surrender to the alpha dog" and conscious "hanging is a judicial procedure." Our subconscious drives aren't well set up to contemplate down the road or abstract consequences. In general people don't submit to justice when they fear for their lives, because the fear of execution is also fairly basic and visceral.

Fear of status loss and spousal anger may be visceral enough to drive us to keep our mouths shut. Often, however, we want to roll over and submit to the jaws of the angry spouse.

The fear of divorce court, financial hardship, and visitation may be too abstract to drive us.

The power of tradition

Throughout history we have been told to "obey our conscience." In a way that's not a bad thing. It means we should be willing to pay taxes to ensure that others can eat or have shelter, that we give to charity and pay for an army for common defense.

However, much of what our conscience does is tell us when we are about to piss off the alpha dog enough to get run out of the pack or attacked. And that means that a lot of our conscience is all in favor of giving in to authority. That may keep us out of trouble. But it's no surprise that the Church, which has throughout history been the right hand of the King or the established social order, wants us to listen to our conscience. It's the seat not only of charity (don't eat more than our share) but obedience (don't anger the alpha). Our conscience isn't magical or religious and it isn't always our friend, though it can help us recognize danger and know when to back down.

Marriage was good for agriculture and society. Kings and nobles might have several mistresses, but it was best if working people got one woman apiece with strict rules not to fight over them. That kept the tax revenue coming in. Understand now why there have always been different rules about cheating for the upper class?

Even in the Democratic 20th Century, the authorities conjectured that having one woman per man was a good idea. Even as Warren G. Harding was being sworn into office while his mistress, Nan Britton waited in the wings, the Film Code was being hatched, mandating that no film should show extramarital sex go unpunished. For five decades American movies could not show an adulterous affair in which there was not a punishment at the end. Even today most "mainstream" and "family" media shies away from unpunished affairs.

Is this because all affairs end in disaster? No. But people whose imaginations are fueled by the idea that they do are more likely to be conformist citizens and have a conscience that stops or sabotages them.

Fortunately there is now media, and culture, that present extramarital affairs without punishment. If you find yourself being pinned on the horns of your conscience, understanding the nature of our inner voices may help.

Be aware when you watch movies or shows (and there are a lot of them) where adultery is punished that you may have the "pangs of conscience." Immunize yourself by treating yourself to a little James Bond who kept himself busy with "three married women" when he was home in London.

Scent

We've already hit very heavily on the core concepts here, so we'll just recap. We believe that in a very high percentage of the cases where a spouse "knows cheating is going on" without any formal proof, the thing which tipped her off is scent. Her partner smelled wrong. She may not even have realized it consciously, but the secret scents of sex and other woman started her mind grinding on infidelity.

- She's more sensitive to scents than you.
- She's sensitive to scents you cannot smell.
- Neither you or she need to be able to smell a scent for it to impact her unconscious mind.
- Other "telltale" scents such as smoke, alcohol, or dance sweat may give away that you have not been where you claimed to be.

Don't bring things contaminated by another woman's perfume, sex, or fluids home for her to smell. Wash yourself. If you can't wash, try to mask the scent with something strong (fresh orange, peanut butter) until you can shower and get your clothes rinsed.

Stay away from sex in your marriage bed. If you must have sex with your partner where your spouse sleeps, come up with an excuse to clean the sheets.

Lube

Men have this tendency to assume that women who want them are wet, willing, and waiting. Many women's bodies are not lube factories. Just as you may ejaculate quite a lot, or not very much, women's lubrication may vary based on time of month, their own biochemistry, or other reasons. Many women who are otherwise ready and willing don't lubricate well.

Stress may also be a factor. A woman may be very nervous about cheating and that may lead to a lack of lube as her body tries to head her off at the pass. Most adult stores sell lube in convenient packets. Avoid the flavored stuff, or anything silicone based. You want water based lube. These days even CVS carries several brands of acceptable lube.

Have it available, and don't take it as an insult if you need some. Lubricated condoms can also help, but don't count on the lube on a condom for comfortable intercourse.

Third parties

Third parties are an almost uncontrollable element. Being seen where you are not supposed to be, by people certain to repeat it to your wife. The best you can do is a sort of controlled crash that might help alleviate the damage. To some extent it depends on how circumstantial. Being seen near your office with a woman of business years is less bad than being spotted by your wife's stylist, poolside in Acapulco, with a 21 year old.

- Plan for this eventuality with your date, and make sure she knows the plan
- Don't act alarmed
- Introduce your date as if it was the most natural thing in the world. Include a minor reference "This is Didi, she's our new contractor for systems security."
- Mention that you saw the so and sos while you were having dinner. Let your wife ask "with who" and answer "oh with Didi, our new analyst. David Parker was there but he only stayed for drinks so I got to do the honors.

- Run scared the next few weeks. The alarm bells have gone off.

Birth control

Birth control can burn you in a dozen ways. Here is the core issue. If you impregnate a woman with your child, unless she is also married, it's a big problem. Even then it may be a big problem, if she considers that grounds to leave her husband, if the child might not resemble him, if she feels she should get an abortion, etc.

The flip side is that most of us don't like condoms, and if we have one regular partner, we may be inclined to skip them, and she may be enthusiastic about that. In fact, despite the trope that it is always the man who wants to skip the condom, in fact it is often the woman who prefers that the condom sit it out. A lot of women can feel ejaculation, and it may be a powerful part of their sexual experience or a trigger for their orgasm.

Which leaves us depending on her for birth control.

Don't depend on any sort of calculated method, no matter how accurate. "Vatican Roulette" is pretty much a guarantee of paternity sooner or later.

Find out as much as you can about her birth control. Many girls are solidly on it, and have no intention of going off it. Some are horrified at the idea of it.

If you don't plan on having any more children you could get a vasectomy. The idea is threatening to a lot of men, but it has little impact on your sex life. Downside: It may be difficult to conceal from, or explain to, your wife.

Pregnancy

There's no positive in pregnancy from an affair. Even on the serial monogamy plan it pushes up the timetable and ensures a messy divorce.

The best case scenario is that you quietly pay for an abortion. Few relationships survive that, and many girls aren't interested. Don't start by putting that on the table, let her take the lead.

Let's be clear. Most women do not intend to trap men into pregnancy.

That said. The pool of attractive girls dating married men may be above average unstable and desperate, not because it's inherently a bad idea but because our culture does not condone or reward it, and people who go against cultural norms are often the ones who are most driven.

Women have a drive towards pregnancy. It's part of their biological norm. They can subvert it, but just as it may not be as satisfying to have sex with a condom even if "it feels just the same," the intellect gets involved.

Many girls who appear to cruelly trap men are probably just acting on unconscious urges. It's hard to understand someone methodically "forgetting" birth control as an unconscious urge, but in fact it's a behavior we see in alcoholics, who are capable of sort of dividing their minds, and working towards sobriety on one track, while subverting themselve, planning to obtain liquor, and constructing situations that lead to exposure to alcohol where short term urges can drive the person to drink. We imagine we're of one mind, but in fact we are all of many minds and those minds don't always work in harmony. The fact is the condom probably *doesn't* actually feel different, but your subconscious is happy to tell you it does if it makes it more likely you'll impregnate someone. And she doesn't mean to miss birth control...it's just that...you get the picture.

If a girl seems to be veering towards pregnancy, you may need to break off the affair. Or have a very serious sober talk. Just remember you're talking with her logical mind. Her unconscious mind may have very different ideas.

Forgetting birth control, pregnancy scares, etc are all problematic. You may want to obtain Plan B contraceptive for use after the fact if she confesses to an "accident." Plan B is an emergency contraceptive known as the "morning after pill." It's available legally, and can now be purchased by men on store shelves. Be aware it's not particularly pleasant, so it shouldn't be a routine plan for birth control. You can also order it online.

There is not yet any effective form of male birth control other than vasectomy, however Vasalgel is expected to become available in 2018. One injection would last for about a year, and be undetectable.

If a woman does become pregnant, we both know you probably want her to get an abortion. However hitting her out of the blue with it is not the best plan. Talk her through the steps and let her talk herself around to it. You may need to carefully indulge in a little fantasy planning in which you give up everything to be with her. Focus on what she would be giving up to have a baby. Focus on the realities and hardships. And if your partner is not at a place where having your baby and forcing you to divorce would be a bad thing for her, be aware that you are at some risk.

Anecdotally we've heard that there tend to be two "peaks" one in the early 20s, and one around 27 when educated middle class women begin to have a strong obsession with pregnancy. Our conclusion would be that it is a cultural phenomenon, driven by hormones. Life settles down, marriage has happened, and there is a feeling of stability. That might tend to be interpreted by the subconscious mind as "safety" sending signals that it is now desirable to have a child. Given the possibility that late 20's is getting towards the upper end of safe childbearing years in pre-industrial society, you may have a cultural trend that plays into a biological trend.

Disease

In the 1970s and 80s there was promise of a guilt free world of sex. There were no incurable diseases left. The most serious case of VD was a short course of penicillin away from cure.

It is hard to get good medical information. Websites run by legitimate health organizations tend toward caution and paranoia. It's easy to tell people not to have sex. With the election of an anti-science regime in the US in 2016, we can no longer seriously recommend the US CDC as a resource. The WHO (World Health Organization) or Mayo Clinic are better sources. For absolutely reliable information that may not be helpful to people planning to engage in sex which carries some risk, those are reliable sources.

We've found that LGBT activist organizations, sex-positive organizations such as Woodhull Foundation, or health resources designed for the kink and fetish community usually point at the best and most reliable information. Instead of having the luxury of saying "avoid risky behavior," they deal with populations where being able to discern the difference between an infinitesimal risk and a serious risk carries profound implications.

Below is an unofficial summary of some of the more striking information we've found. It is opinion, and condensed from various sources. We suggest you do your own research.

Serious diseases

AIDS

AIDS is the disease that everyone thinks of, though people with AIDS can live a normal lifespan. By now, most everyone understands that it's just another STD, and that you can get it through intercourse with persons of either gender.

Joseph Sebstian

You probably won't run into AIDS having an affair. Most people who have the disease know it, and take it seriously. People with a chance of exposure knew that too. Your chances of contracting AIDS from a partner or hookup are incredibly remote.

Still, AIDS is a thing which can kill you. To dramatically reduce or remove the risk, you may want to consider pre-exposure prophylaxis (PReP) with TRUVADA.

Your doctor may not wish to prescribe you TRUVADA, or your health plan may be reluctant to cover it. Many doctors do not understand or sympathize with the idea of cheating, or going to sex workers (who probably do more testing, and have lower incidence of disease than the rest of the population), or do not fully understand the incidence of AIDS in the heterosexual population. It may be easiest to convince your physician to prescribe TRUVADA if you state that you have homosexual partners.

Major health organizations have been reluctant to estimate the risk of infection from oral sex alone, however it is generally considered very low, especially for the receptive partner. In recent years there has been less emphasis on the use of barriers for oral sex in sex-positive communities, with no significant uptick in AIDS.

Hepatitis

While most people do not regard Hepatitis as an STD, one of the more common modes of the spread of viral hepatitis B is through intimate sexual contact. Sexual transmission is believed to be responsible for a significant percentage of the cases worldwide.

Hep B can be serious or fatal. If you plan on sex with partners you do not know well, ask your doctor for a Hep B vaccination.

Syphilis

Getting oral sex from a partner with a syphilis sore or rash on the lips or mouth, or in the throat, can result in getting syphilis, which is generally curable with antibiotics. Syphilis is serious, but is one of the less dreaded diseases in the modern era. It can be transmitted via oral sex.

Gonorrhea

Gonorrhea is problematic in that it can be transmitted via oral. Until a few years ago it was largely the least important of the diseases. Now there is a strain of antibiotic resistant gonorrhea which must be treated with cephalosporin antibiotics. That's a lot more serious and something to take care for. And yes, resistant gonorrhea can be transmitted via oral sex.

STDs doctors, and the law

Your doctor is going to expect you to inform your wife of your STD. It is likely that your doctor will seek to force you to notify your partner. Reading articles in the AMA Journal of Ethics, doctors may risk ignoring HIPAA if they feel the stakes are high enough.

Most states don't mandate that you tell your partner you have an STD, though New York and a few other states do. No states mandate that your doctor inform your partner.

Let's assume for the sake of argument you are absolutely certain that your wife does not have your STD, for example you have not had sex in many months, since before you began having sex with a new partner.

Your doctor will ask if they can inform the Health Department. They may make you fill out a form that lists your spouse and any other partners before you are tested. In theory they will tell you that the health Department will disclose your condition to your wife and other partners. In practice the Doctor may or may not be completely honest or forthcoming about this.

If you and your wife share a practice, it is possible your Doctor may arrange to inform your wife, directly or indirectly. That's a violation of law, but it might be hard to prove, or your Doctor may care more about medical ethics than the law. One way to avoid this may be to go to clinics that allow for anonymous testing. These exist in most big cities.

Our suggestions

We can't tell you what to do, but not telling your wife about an STD is both unethical and impractical. There could be serious health damage, and if she discovers that she's sick and you have not informed her, there could be a lawsuit or even criminal charges if you have been her only partner.

We suggest that you construct one event to confess to. A
night on the road, an indiscretion. Tell her, explain the
consequences and beg for mercy. At worst, the divorce will
be less ugly.

Embarrassing diseases

HPV

If you're a man under the age of 26, get vaccinated for HPV.

HPV is pretty common infection. About half the population
has had an infection. It is scary because it can be related to
television commercials showing death of cervical cancer. In
practical terms it is endemic, you probably won't know if you
have it, and probably won't know of you transmit it. If your
wife comes down with it, and has had no other partners,
point to literature suggesting that it can be transmitted non-
sexually (debated) and that it can go unrecognized for years.

Herpes

If you have herpes, get treated and don't have sex when
you're able to transmit herpes. Practically speaking you may
need to tell your spouse. That said, herpes is mostly a
nuisance. It can be transmitted through non-sexual contact
which both presents additional risk, and some plausible
deniability.

Trichomoniasis "Trich"

A protozoan that causes a heavy and foul smelling discharge.
It is easily curable, however there's no plausible deniability,

another reason to be careful if you have sex with partners you pick up.

Crabs

Probably the most embarrassing thing to bring home, crabs are usually spread through pubic hair. If you like going down on your partners, they can also infect your eyelids or eyebrows. If you have sex in sketchy circumstances or with sketchy partners, consider keeping a lice-killing shampoo with 1% permethrin content on hand and showering afterwards. You can buy such a shampoo at over the counter at the drugstore, and if you have a safe shower facility can keep it in a locker there. Wash underwear in hot water, or dispose of it.

The good news. A night at a cheap motel is sufficient explanation for crabs. They can (not often) be transmitted by bedding.

Testing

It can be surprisingly difficult to get tested for STDs, especially by your doctor. In theory he or she should be willing to test you if you say you've had partners other than your wife, however this can often go with scolding and lifestyle discussion that makes it problematic. You need to look for a doctor who does not give you problems over testing.

As mentioned there are clinics in many cities, and numerous services now offer private, discreet, testing. Make sure the service you use is well reviewed and reliable.

The hidden damage

One of the most common elements of damage from STDs or STD scares is your marriage. Often people who are engaged in affairs claim that it won't hurt the marriage. Then they have risky sex, and end up icing their spouse out for weeks while they get tested. Even a few sharp turndowns because "I don't feel well" can lead to hard feelings. Balance the fear of giving yourself away with an STD with the need to maintain intimacy in your marriage. Having your wife feel bitter and rejected because you said "no" to her first sexual overture in weeks, when the real reason is that you were waiting for your STD test results, is not helpful to either of you.

Jealousy

Certainly one of the best known problems with affairs is jealousy. Your partner becomes sickly jealous of your wife and insists on having you for herself. Or you believe that your partner should remain faithful to you because you're not "really" involved with your wife anymore.

Jealousy is a powerful and primitive human emotion. If you find yourself falling under its spell, you need to calm down, take a cold shower, and manage your own expectations.

If you find your partner falling under its spell, you may need to pull away sharply before things get dangerous. Jealousy can grow, and early signs of growing jealousy can leave you trapped in a situation you cannot easily get out of.

If a girl you've met for sex once or twice phones your wife about your affair, you may be able to pass it off as wishful thinking. Suggest she got together with you on a pretext and is trying to punish you for rejecting a pass she made. If you've been conducting an affair for a year and a half, the evidence will be overwhelming.

We suggest that if you seriously fear jealousy getting out of hand you pull away. If there is serious fear that she may contact your wife, immunize her by explaining beforehand about her unexpected pass at you.

Marking

We've talked in general terms about the possibility that your affair partner might sabotage your marriage or long term relationship. One way that happens is through marking behaviors.

Marking happens when your partner:

- Marks your body
- Leaves markings (hair, scent, lipstick) on your clothing
- Leaves items of a feminine or sexual nature in your car, house, or another space frequented by your spouse

Let's not get too paranoid here. Not every oversight is marking. She got excited and scratched you. She laid her head on your shoulder and there are hairs. She lost an earring while you were taking her against the car door.

It's your job to police your environment. You can't blame her for your basic oversights. She's not going to want to act as policewoman for your wife's sensibilities.

Watch, especially if it keeps going. We knew one partner who managed to remove and "lose" a full used condom every time she had sex in her partner's home bedroom. Wrappers and other detritus can serve as "markers" A sanitary napkin dropped in the trash can be a marker, or just an accident brought on by a moment of distraction. In any case, check any bathrooms your partner has used, including the trash, as well as the bedroom, and any other rooms.

Marking is probably an unconscious behavior, and some people are just forgetful or careless, especially when aroused and distracted. A higher than normal level of debris can mean that her unconscious mind is out to leave "marks" that make you hers, and alienate your regular partner.

Pushing to have sex in the bed where you sleep with your wife may be a marking behavior. It may also just be enjoying a bit of taboo one-upsmanship. The two are closely related. See if the behavior is continued or compulsive.

What to do?

Usually when it comes to human beings we recommend talking, however we've never known a woman to be receptive to discussing her own "marking" behaviors. Usually she really doesn't know she is doing them, and the conversation reminds her of everything she is not getting out of the affair.

We've already discussed how to be safe.

- Don't meet at a space your spouse has access to.
- Don't transport your partner in your own car.
- Shower and change afterwards.

Of course that's not always practical. The best you can do is avoid head on problems and avoid head on collisions.

Don't fuck in your own bed. If you do, clean the sheets which is problematic in itself...when did you ever clean the sheets? Buying two sets of identical new sheets can help, but again that can be problematic...when did you ever buy sheets?

Keeping affair sex to the recreation room or a downstairs couch can give you longer to find any debris, and give your wife less chance of stumbling across evidence. Don't forget to police guest bathrooms, your own car, etc.

Most car wash places have a pay by coin vacuum. Running this around the passenger seat, driver's seat, the back if you used it for sex, and the cracks of her seat can help make sure anything you didn't see still gets sucked away to oblivion.

Easily checked deceptions

This should follow from everything else we have written here, but it is such a common issue it deserves an entry of its own. *Avoid easily checked lies.* "I dropped by your sister's house" works only if it is never discussed. This is the sort of lie that could easily unravel by accident, and is certain to explode if there is the faintest suspicion.

It is actually better to have no good lie at all than one which can easily be checked. It is often seen as an emotional trade off. "I fell asleep in my car" is strange and likely to cause suspicion. "I dropped by your sister's house" seems very likely. Yet the one leads only to suspicion and the other to disaster if it is not confirmed.

Once in a great while you may need to roll the dice on an easily checked lie. Remember that they stack up, and if it passes easily and is never questioned, don't let that make you think it never will be. Eventually disaster will occur.

Easily checked lies are usually a result of laziness, or a guilty conscience that tells you that "planning for an affair" is evil and that letting it happen and then making up lies off the cuff is "more moral." That way lies disaster. Your mind is taking the easy route around your conscience. Let lust carry you through then make up a story in the aftermath when the consequences are much harsher. That way you never have to face the question "why do it at all."

Lay your groundwork. Plan. You are going to do this thing. It is better to do it seamlessly and without hurting anyone than messily in a way that involves others and brings you ruin.

We recommend that you cook up one or two "emergency" all purpose excuses. Sudden work trips are good, but car breakdowns, requests from an old (nonexistent) High School buddy for help, taking a (trusted) friend to detox or a meeting because they fell off the wagon....have a few good stories waiting. Examine them from every angle and make sure they

don't have weak spots. Use those if you really get into
trouble.

Emergencies

From time to time something really bad will happen. You
break a leg in Las Vegas while you were supposed to be in St.
Paul. You have a heart attack in her bed and she calls 911.
She has a heart attack in your house. You get in a car
accident where she was driving your car.

Hospitals

If she gets sick, you'll at least be able to make phone calls and
keep yourself "on the radar." This is where a prepped excuse
(surprise business trip, friend in recovery) can really pay off.
Bear in mind that abandoning her can cause problems, but so
can being around for her family to show up. If possible, talk
to her about what she wants. Passing you off as "a fellow
diner who saw her fall" or "a friend of my boss" might work.
A gallant but ultimately platonic friend. Don't seem too
concerned or too interested, especially if she is married.

If it is you that has an accident, this may be the moment your
affair is exposed. There are a few things you can do if you do
a lot of affairs outside your relationship. One is to remove
your wife from your emergency contacts and replace her with
a trusted confederate. For relationship you can put "cousin"
or "brother in law" as that's almost impossible to prove...after
all you wouldn't have the same last name. This needs to be
someone who owes you enough to bail your ass out and help
you come up with an excuse. It may be no big deal if you're
cheating in the same town "yeah I fell down on the squash

court," or a very big deal if you were in Cancun when you were supposed to be in Biloxi.

Have a plan. For any major out of town trip, have a plan for what's going on. It may be better to construct a work conference in Cancun, than to plead a trip to Boise, then explain why you're in a Mexican hospital.

Cars

While things are changing in the modern days of dash cams, if it is your car you should be driving it. If you aren't because (for example) you were drunk and she was sober, you are going to have quite a bit of explaining to do. Still, provided you intercept the mail, most claims are handled online these days.

If police get involved or there is a DUI, you may be in deeper shit. The police are under no obligation not to tell the spouse who comes to bail you out that you had a passenger, even if they let her go free.

Avoid doing things in cars that expose you to risk. Uber has its own issues and can be tracked but only if you're a fool and the bank account for your linked card, or your phone is available to your spouse. Overall if drinking is involved you're safer with transportation that doesn't involve any sort of risk.

Devices

Test Strips and UV Lights

A company called CheckMate sells test strips to test underwear for semen. They put this forward as producing evidence if your spouse is cheating by evidence left in their underwear. Ridiculous of course. After all, there are many things other than cheating that could cause that. Masturbation, or even simple arousal with fluid discharge can leave traces of semen.

Still, it's just more reason to keep your cheating laundry and your worn laundry separate. But you might not think to change underwear. It's important that you do so. You can wash underwear in a sink, or buy a spare pack and occasionally run underwear, socks, and t-shirts at an actual laundromat, or when your spouse isn't home.

Other companies sell UV lights for semen stain detection. These are more likely to embarrass you for wanking than catch a cheater, but they're annoying all the same.

Other devices

There are also GPS trackers that can be hidden in your car (as could a phone) or attached magnetically to the underside, as well as dozens of models of spy camera that could be left in your house or car. These are no longer far-fetched purchases. They cost less than $50 (often less than $30) and can be obtained from Amazon.

Know the divorce laws

Finally, know the divorce laws in your state. What makes your property most vulnerable? Do you want custody? If not, how much will you need to pay in support?

We can't provide legal advice, but we can condense some points made by Katherine Eisold Miller, a collaborative lawyer and family mediator. writing in Huffington Post

Miller says that in the current day, adultery rarely has much impact on how assets are divided up, though she warns of situations where an actual asset was used to support the adultery. For example, if you sold a jointly owned boat to pay for your trip to Cancun, or put a second mortgage on your jointly owned house to support putting your partner up in a student apartment, you'd probably be liable for compensating your wife by losing some other assets.

Miller also says that as long as you haven't exposed your children to anyone inappropriate, or carried on the affair in front of them, adultery doesn't usually affect custody.

Fault isn't a factor in divorce in every state, though even where a state has no-fault divorce. Miller suggests that in states with fault-based divorce proven adultery can have an effect on the division of property or on court-ordered support. Proven adultery can also reduce the obligation of a spouse to pay alimony, even if the other party needs it. Usually alimony is terminated when your ex-spouse moves in with someone else, so parting on good terms so you can set her up with your friends is always a good idea.

If you give your spouse an STD, you can be sued for personal injury. Miller tells us this is called an interspousal tort.

Most importantly, says Miller, adultery tends to encourage divorces to settlement. Sheepish spouses (that's you) want to prove they aren't so bad, and are faced with an angry spouse. You may tend to "give up" more at the table than you meant to, or would have if the divorce were amicable and fair. She suggests that separating your feelings from your actions is the best course to making good long term decisions in divorce.

Check with a local lawyer or the web to see if your state has no-fault divorce.

Down the road

The long game

Where is this all going? If you aren't hunting for the next Mrs. Right, how do you plan to live in harmony with the current Mrs. Right? How do you intend to pass your affair off as the caution of a spy gives way to the blase assumption that you can't get caught? There are a number of ontologies.

Just a friend

In some circumstances, particularly if your wife has male friends, you can pass off a female friend as platonic. You travel, perhaps for a hobby, or work, and your wife steadfastly believes you have no interest in her. This can be a strain if she and your wife spend much time together, as lack of permission to touch you grates on her and reminds her of her second class status. This works best if you're both married.

I am a secret agent

You find secrecy and procedures easy and despite a burgeoning amount of stuff to keep track of, you keep everything cleanly sorted out, never compromising your legend. Anais Nin was involved in cheating so complex she carried an index card box on transcontinental flights to remind herself what her actual stories were with each partner.

Where does the road lead?

In the end, where are you going with your affair? Ultimately all options boil down to four basic possibilities

- I have affairs and don't maintain them very long.
- I want to turn the affair into your primary relationship, divorce, marry my affair partner.
- I eventually want to push my partner into polyamory and make my affair "open."
- I want an affair that runs stably for years. One other person is all I can handle.
- I want to maintain my young affair until she starts to age a little, then trade her for a younger model, while never giving up my wife.

Those are the options. Be honest with yourself about them and you'll be happier, and less problematic.

Your wife

She tolerates it

Another common pattern is that after some period of time, the certainty of an affair just creeps into the relationship. This is not always a bad thing. Harvard Psychologist Daniel Gilbert explains why we get upset about terrorists but not global warming.

"Because we barely notice changes that happen gradually, we accept gradual changes that we would reject if they happened abruptly. The density of Los Angeles traffic has increased dramatically in the last few decades, and citizens have tolerated it with only the obligatory grumbling. Had that change happened on a single day last summer, Angelenos would have shut down the city, called in the National Guard and lynched every politician they could get their hands on."

If the dawning awareness of your affairs is a slow creeping certainty that progresses from "could it be" to "of course" without ever uncovering a smoking gun, you may pass into that comfortable situation where "she knew about father's affairs of course, and pretended not to."

That's not really a comfortable place. It means you have latitude and with the right woman may even have some enjoyment at home. But she still resents you, and resents the attention you have withdrawn, and resent is poisonous.

Quid Pro Quo

Another possible situation is one where she also cheats. This can, occasionally, work out. The trick is why she is cheating. If it's out of resentment and a need to prove herself, it may work poorly. If she is really into it, and is getting a strong high off the new relationship, she may be willing to agree to most anything to have you give it your blessing.

In that case, *do not announce you are also having an affair.* That moment of relief will cost you. Point out that you've had offers, and...you might be okay with her acting on hers if she is willing to let you act on yours.

Congratulations, you've made a messy, emergency conversion to polyamory. Start reading up on resources soon (see above) and don't assume your partner wants to be BFFs with your wife just because your wife has said it's okay.

Sometimes a sort of Victorian Quid Pro Quo can prevail where you both cheat but neither actually says anything about it. For some couples, especially those with another strong interest that binds them to each other, this can work.

Try to keep it humorous rather than poisonous. Friendly jokes and slight winks along with a loving hug and a kiss...reassurances of everlasting care...can make this situation less toxic.

Glaciation

In the end, it is hard for an affair not invite the creep of glaciers over a relationship. Maybe the glaciers were already moving in, but they will get colder. Secrets mount up. Missed personal time mounts up. Grievances over kids or other issues mount up. Lack of sex mounts up. Being aware of those things can allow you to offset glaciation, but not entirely stop it. Be aware and consider where you want your life to be. If you want two full, rich, relationships, it will take a lot of work. If you want sex without the hassle of a divorce, you are merely marking time.

Checklists and Conclusion

Readiness checklist

    __ Know why you're cheating
    __ Resolve any guilt issues and get yourself into mental
shape
    __ Secure PC
    __ Secure locked Phone
    __ Secure Phone Number (Google Voice)
    __ Secure Email Address
    __ Secure/alternate Social media
    __ Where to look for partners
    __ Explanation for taking money, or way to conceal it
    __ Way to get the money you have gotten and spend it
without complications
    __ If searching online, have a good profile
    __ Lay groundwork for excuses before you need them

Per date checklist

    __ Grooming
        __ Hair
        __ Clothing
        __ Scent
    __ Conversation ideas - know her
    __ Anecdotes
    __ Location for changing (if applicable)
    __ Location for date
    __ Location for sex

___ Location for cleanup
___ Transportation plans
___ Money planned in advance
___ Contraception/Protection
___ Lube
___ Sanitize
    ___ Clothes
    ___ Skin
    ___ Car or room (if applicable)
___ Excuse for your time away
___ Know your legend

Conclusion

The world is a changing place. Agrarian or Victorian morality is breaking down, and we are slowly moving into an era of individualism and sexual freedom, when we will make our own choices. It is likely that few of us are really happy with only one person in our lives.

We hope this book provides a way to be more socially responsible about the legal adult decision to engage in infidelity, while conveying the responsibility and pitfalls. In the end we hope it creates more happiness in the world and less misery and sadness.

The world is not Hollywood. The couple getting back together is not always the happy ending. Faithfulness unto death is not always the happy ending. We are adults and we need writing and instruction that speaks to the real, sophisticated, complex, world we inhabit.

Review Us

Joseph Sebastian and his team worked hard to bring you this guide to cheating. A lot of ebooks out there are "fly by night" and don't give you real, detailed, information. Or they tell you what you want to hear, rather than explaining the dangers and difficulties. If you think we've been honest, detailed and useful, please consider reviewing this book on Amazon.

We expect this book to be under reviewed, because we know a lot of you can't. But if you bought this book on a burner account, or you got a divorce anyway, or your spouse never uses Amazon, float us a few stars.

Help us by deciding right now on a time and place you're going to write an Amazon review of this book. Tomorrow morning after you have coffee at your office. Tomorrow night as soon as your spouse is asleep. Help us if we've helped you.

Thank you for reading.
And Good Luck, whatever your choices.

www.ingramcontent.com/pod-product-compliance
Lightning Source LLC
Chambersburg PA
CBHW050129280326
41933CB00010B/1299